THERE ARE NO GODS *in* NORTH KOREA

THERE ARE NO GODS *in* NORTH KOREA

ANJALY THOMAS

NIYOGI BOOKS

Published by
NIYOGI BOOKS
D-78, Okhla Industrial Area, Phase-I
New Delhi-110 020, INDIA
Tel: 91-11-26816301, 49327000
Fax: 91-11-26810483, 26813830
email: niyogibooks@gmail.com
website: www.niyogibooksindia.com

Editor: Sucharita Ghosh
Design: Shashi Bhushan Prasad

ISBN: 978-93-85285-33-2
Publication: 2016

Printed at: Niyogi Offset Pvt. Ltd., New Delhi, India

For Nitin Shukla. Who always believes in doing things.

But really what can I say about someone who gives me the wings to fly and energy to keep me on my toes…

Who doesn't flinch when I talk of 'things I want to do…'

Who knows me to be a work-in-progress cook and yet looks forward to dinner every night…

Who gives me a dozen when I ask for two…

Who is always my first source of information, news and comfort. Whose love for life blows me off my feet every day…

To you I say this—In this vast universe it is a pleasure to spend my life with you.

And because of you…I am unafraid.

CONTENTS

THERE ARE NO GODS IN NORTH KOREA

I have been to the Democratic People's Republic of Korea, or North Korea, according to the media, much to the dissatisfaction of the Koreans. I am not sure there are a lot of people who can say so and I might have pissed off a few people just by saying this, as I am sure I will the few North Koreans with access to internet who probably will read this sometime.

And oh, it wasn't easy or cheap but it was, I say with pride, worth it.

But here is how it all began.

For the purpose of safeguarding the identity of the sender of this email, I will call him Mr Man Machine.

Dear Anjaly

I did not know you were a travel writer; it's very difficult to take in writers/journalists into North Korea. These are not our rules. These are the rules put in place by the North Korean government, they can also check at times by using Google on passenger's names and profession.

Please, can you send me some links or information about yourself? Also is this your main job? Please follow the link to these related rules for North Korea.

To protect the guides we work with, passengers and our ground staff we always ask passengers to sign a disclaimer stating that the reason for travel is tourism and articles will not be published. However in certain situations we can take in writers. Please advice.

The two most unpopular profiles you could have, if you were hopeful of visiting DPRK, are that of a preacher and a writer. I was in the latter category. The short mail brought my dreams to a grinding halt. My yearning to visit what the Western media called the Hermit Kingdom would never materialise because I was a writer. I did not know if I should feel proud or angry or both but that depended on who I was narrating my plight to—but it seemed that North Korea, the Holy Grail of the newshounds worldwide, would remain forever out of my reach.

Damn.

There was nothing wrong with being a writer in the rest of the world but the law makers of DPRK didn't think so. They had made out writers to be the scum of the earth, a kind that existed with the sole purpose of maligning a nation of pure-breeds such as themselves, painting gruesome pictures of starvation when in reality their leaders were true incarnations of gods.

But I also happened to know that liberty in DPRK was a joke but that is exactly what aroused my curiosity. I was eager to know more about the country ruled by a portly young leader Kim Jong-Un whose play things included nuclear missiles. KJU also happened to love cheese, wine and sports and when not indulging in his peculiar hobby of dashing off to the sun, ruled the country with an iron hand, a trait inherited from the eternal president Kim Il Sung dead since 1972. His particular dislike of the Americans is a legacy of his forefathers, but somehow, journalists, photographers, religious preachers, South Koreans and freedom for their countrymen got added to the hate-list.

Yes, you can see why I was curious. Hey, I was a journalist once.

If I could somehow convince Mr Man Machine that my true reason to enter DPRK was to fulfil a traveller's curiosity and that I had no mischief up my sleeve whatsoever, I could gain entry. Maybe. It was a chance worth taking. In the coming days, I prepared my traveller's resume, scanned Google for every bit of information about me and finding nothing self-incriminatory, emailed back the links that I thought would prove my innocence and prayed hard.

Let me clarify that I do not blame Mr Man Machine or his Beijing-based company run mostly by the British, because I believe they were doing their best. They listened earnestly. They tried their best to understand and find a middle ground. This is the thing about dealing with professionals who were also not Chinese—they listened and they understood. They did not shut the door on you if they didn't like your face; or, in my case, profession.

Few weeks of finger-crossing and fervent praying later something happened—perhaps the gods of DPRK smiled. Or mine. I can't be sure, but I'd lean towards mine. There were no gods in DPRK. There were The Kims and it was somehow the same thing.

'We might be able to take you in,' Mr Man Machine replied.

Definitely my God. *Amen.*

In his email were links to a website that contained in many lengthy pages of serious text everything a tourist had to know about DPRK, including the dos and don'ts. To be fair, the webpages containing the dos were not as lengthy or grim as the section on don'ts without explaining why, but I will let that pass. What could an innocent tourist do that could offend the Democratic People's Republic of Korea?

As it stands, plenty.

I was ready to sign any document assuring Mr Man Machine my complete cooperation with the local guides in Pyongyang and tolerance for any discrimination I might be subjected to, patience, respect and obedience to the regime. All this was required of me, but I was okay with that as long as I was allowed entry. I would be ignorant on purpose and enjoy the show and embrace deception—which is unlike me, but I figured it would be easier to go with the flow when visiting North Korea.

I suppose as long as I was allowed to talk, take pictures and eat local food, I would survive. Only as I read through the don'ts it became clear that striking up conversations with locals was a sure way to get arrested or deported and worse, cause the guide and the said local to be arrested.

There were many things I did not understand—why it was okay to use American currency but it was not okay to flash American brands or carry a GPS-enabled phone into the country. But if that was what it took to gain entry into DPRK, then that is what I would do. My intention was not to create trouble for myself or others, least of all myself.

And clever, smart travellers know how to play the game. If I had to read everything about the Juche philosophy or eat kimchi with a smile, I would.

I am a thoughtful traveller like that.

Not a lot of people thought very much of my DPRK trip. The geographically challenged ones mixed it up with South Korea and wished me a happy holiday, some put forward moral objections to the trip and few wished me luck not really caring much. Well, people were like that—especially the non-travellers who lacked the fire inside. They were everywhere too. That was the danger.

But five people had positive things to say although they began their sentence with something totally negative about the place and my determination but redeemed themselves by adding their inputs, patting my back and wishing me luck to see this through. If I insisted on going to my own execution, they were not going to throw a spanner in my works.

One of five was my dad. The second was Nitin, the love of my life. The third was a journalist friend. The fourth and the fifth were my brothers. And all of them seemed to know a little more about DPRK than I did and because the approval of five people I hold dear outweighed the opinions of the hundreds of acquaintances, I knew I was going to be all right.

That said, the final mail of approval came three weeks before the said tour commenced and the days preceding that was a flurry of emails, multiple level cross-checks and fund transfers, but I had an assurance.

I also had an alternative profession to flaunt, although fake. If anyone asked, I would pretend to be a kindergarten teacher—a supremely noble profession and one that no one had anything against.

You gotta give it to the British—they do think of the nicest professions when needed. Even my over-imaginative mind could not have conceived a better and safer profession to gain entry. Who would ever suspect a nice kindergarten teacher such as myself?

As I packed my shorts and tees, I wondered if I was expected to dress the part.

My North Korean Bubble burst during the pre-tour briefing in Beijing, the day before departure. The entire lot of tourists going on the July tour had read the rules and signed on the dotted lines, but as the tour coordinators explained the rules, some twice, following them up with examples, North Korea seemed more sinister than the media made it out to be and the sixty of us felt like the stupid moths flapping around the flame looking forward to dying.

'These five days are going to change your lives forever,' said the tour coordinator in a serious attempt at humour. 'Grab your last Starbucks coffee at the airport, eat your muffins and croissants, get enough money for the trip, in small change if possible, and never try to speak to the locals.'

She touched upon every possible subject connected to the trip—everything from flight meals to taking photographs, bowing at statues, staying 'in-line', always checking with the guide about the repercussions of folding or damaging a newspaper containing pictures of the ruler.

'If there is anything that will get you arrested or deported, it is damaging the picture of the Great Leaders,' they told us over and over again. 'Always keep any piece of paper with the Great Leader intact.'

Arrest was the solution to everything in North Korea.

Much of the North Korean animosity, it appeared, was directed at the Americans, so there was a good half hour dedicated to American behaviour in North Korea. What the tour coordinators worried about was the American temper that was likely to get out of hand upon hearing the Korean version of The War and the subsequent surrender of America and the general slandering of the rest of the world. I think India did not fall into this category so there was no reason to dedicate time to this. I also happened to know that India shared a good relationship with DPRK and shipped food grains to contain the famine from time to time.

'No matter what, grin and bear it,' continued the tour coordinator. 'No matter how angry you are or how much you want to clear your country's good name or the history in general, remember you are in their country. Remember they have been kind enough to let you in, so that says a lot.

'Remember, your guide is not ill-informed or at fault for telling you their version of the war. They are duty bound to carry out instructions. They tell you what they believe, err, have grown up to believe in. Give them some space. Just remember to check with them before you do anything—and yeah, they would be happy to receive a gift, like cigarettes and chocolates.'

And as a parting shot—'Guys, please get yourself a tie or a pant if you will—and a shirt. One of our itinerary demands it… and ladies, a below-the-knee dress. And preferably no exposing the shoulders or, umm, too much of the neck.'

As we filed out of the room, I was convinced that all sixty of us did have a rather twisted sense of adventure and were secretly proud to be the chosen few to get into North Korea.

But the last piece of news on North Korea brought to us via *The Guardian,* as we were ready to board Air Koryo the next morning, depressed me. The article reported that North Korean farmers were under great amounts of pressure to grow more crops to feed a hungry nation while the portly Kim Jong-Un had declared that North Korea would never have to tighten its belts again.

As I read through the article, KJU's optimistic declaration seemed to be the only piece of good news and I had an increasing feeling of uneasiness and many questions about going hungry on the trip.

To be fair, had I been airdropped without the knowledge of where, I'd have found the scenery very captivating. Endless fields of rice, peaceful rivers and green hills all the way to the horizon and if it weren't for the mountains that crept in here and there ruining the picture perfect scenery, I'd have given the scenery a huge thumbs up.

But I knew where I was. I did however make a brave attempt to block out that knowledge for a fleeting moment so I could enjoy what was really a magical stretch of green, but that knowledge ruined the magic unfolding below.

The ugly, uneaten burger sitting on my pull-out table was a reminder that I was indeed in Korean airspace so I alternated between glancing outside and peering over the shoulder of my co-passenger and trip-mate, at the *Pyongyang Times* he was reading in amusement.

The front page was fully devoted to the Beloved Leader Kim Jong-Un and his visit to the orphanage and a large picture of happy children surrounding the leader. The inside, however, had a few interesting bits—it was enlightening to know of the technological advancements the country had made and how they were ready to take on the world, namely America, Japan and South Korea.

I could contain myself no longer. I hissed into my neighbour's ear.

'What the hell is all that? How ridiculous.'

He had the good sense to look over his shoulders quickly before whispering back—

'Damned if I know what to make of it. It's a load of crap.'

And you can guess where he came from. I would see red too—if, first thing in the morning my eyes fell upon false propaganda against my country. I'd grit my teeth and make a fist and want to throw punches too—so he was within his rights to hiss and clench his fist and make a feeble attempt to crumple the newspaper.

'I feel like a traitor not reacting,' he said, growing redder, 'but I guess Uncle Sam will appreciate my position.'

I myself was posing as a kindergarten teacher and kindergarten teachers had a certain behavioural pattern that did not include showing outright agitation.

'Well, you got me there,' I said instead. 'It's a good read though.'

On the fringes of the runway three old Air Koryo planes sat motionless, secured to the ground with thick ropes. Heavy tarps covered the cockpits. Grass grew around their wheels. It was the first indication that something was not right. Why were these old planes displayed like that?

Between getting off the plane and walking towards the old, functional airport, Katarzyna caught up with me. We had spoken briefly at Beijing airport and hurriedly exchanged names but I had a feeling we were going to get along very well.

'I am feeling weird, you know,' she said, 'I cannot believe I am here.'

That somehow heightened the discomfort I was feeling too.

'Breathe,' I said, more to myself than to her. 'Breathe.'

Meanwhile the other passengers were not exactly holding out well, each throwing meaningful and furtive glances at each other as though preparing for something to happen. It was as if every one of us had created ominous scenarios in our heads and were hoping some of that might come true.

We entered the small building. Kim Il Sung and Kim Jong-Il or simply The Kims smiled at us from the walls across the immigration desk.

I have been through small and very small airports before. In fact, I love airports. I love going through them—to me, it is a hallway to something fascinating beyond. This airport was smallish, yes, but it was also in a state of chaos.

There were no real lines, only a large number of unsure people jumping queues. We had filled out our details on two pieces of paper listing all of our personal belongings, including books, radios, mobile phones and cameras. It was funny how our baggage was scanned on the way out of the containment area.

All of us made it out of the airport without any fuss.

From here on, I will refer to our local guides with different names and offer muted opinions or omit details that might put others, particularly the locals we deal with, in any kind of risk.

Our local guides, aka, minders were waiting on the other side.

We were introduced to Miss Deer.

Miss Deer was beautiful. She had flawless skin. She wore a knee length skirt. And she spoke excellent English. She was beautiful. She would have to be, I learnt later, because she lived in Pyongyang and for that one had to be beautiful. Living in Pyongyang was an honour given to the selected two million. She was beautiful and fit the bill in every way.

Miss Deer was to be our guide, along with Li the driver, Li the-other-guide and Li the-minder-of-Miss Deer and Li the-other-guide. I will call Li the-other-guide Giraffe because he was too tall for a Korean.

'This is going to get very interesting,' Katarzyna whispered once we boarded the bus and took the backseat. 'This country is full of Lis, I think. This is so funny. You think it's their real name? Li, Li, Li…' Katarzyna made that into a little tune, she was funny that way. I put it down to Polish humour.

'Nah, I don't think so. But at least they had the good sense to choose an easy one. Weird that we end up with three on this tour…they could have split them with the other groups, no?'

As we waited for the others to board and settle down, we snapped pictures of the airport behind us and a few buildings around that were under construction. Like any first time visitor into any country, everything was interesting, including buildings under construction.

Miss Deer quickly stopped us.

'It is forbidden to take pictures of building under construction,' she said in her beautiful voice. 'We Koreans see it as something unfinished, so no photos please.'

See, how she had used the word 'forbidden' and not something less scary? It would have been hilarious at this point, but that was also when we were asked to hand over our passports 'for your own safety'—and nothing was funny any more.

I am not sure I understood how turning my passport over to the guides ensured my safety.

In the minutes following this, everyone was quiet—perhaps all of us, the Americans, Germans, Poles (Katarzyna or Kate as I called her), a Slovenian, Dutch, Singaporean, Australian and I, the odd Indian, had the same thought.

Hence, with my fear of going hungry came another fear.

What if they lost my passport and I was stuck here forever?

I hoped these thoughts wouldn't get in the way of enjoying the rest of the stay. Kate thought the same, bless her.

Soon we were joined by another, unexpected man. Let's call him Mr Videoman, a short man with unsmiling eyes who carried a big, outdated video camera on his shoulder, like the ones you see in village weddings. We were told that he would record our trip so that in the end we could purchase a DVD from him as a present.

He could have been anything, even a spy, or it could be our imagination on an overdrive, but he was on board and he was there to stay.

FOR YOUR OWN SAFETY

The ride to the city was smooth and from the air-conditioned tour bus Pyongyang looked like any other peaceful city. And clean—with the exception of soldiers who were everywhere, with guns, watching over local people who attended to lawns, trimmed hedges, crawled on their knees to cut grass with small knives and swept streets. Briefly my mind went back to my home country—a sight like this would have been a welcome change. Pyongyang could be a good example of cleanliness. If only…

In the short ride to Arch of Triumph, our first stop—the lines had been drawn, introductions made—we formed a fair opinion on who was going to get along with whom. Under the Arch, new friendships were formed and while the minders and guides blurred history and facts with stories of the Great Leader and his conquests I got acquainted with Larry, the tall American and his partner Valerie Menenberg.

Among the lots of us, it was easy to guess who was what—from the way they held their cameras, from the pictures they took, their expressions when the guides spun yarns, their interest in the guide-talk, questions asked and the final giveaway—from the way they dressed.

I hate to sound like some kind of a behavioural expert, but you could tell.

Larry had travelled a lot. In fact, he was on a world trip with Valerie and you could see from his manner that he had seen much. He also knew about monuments. He pointed at the one I was photographing and said—

'Did you know this is the exact replica of the Arch of Triumph in Paris, this one is definitely taller, but it's otherwise the same, only less impressive?'

I did not. So I raised an eyebrow, smiled a little and said, 'Really? Oh! Looks impressive enough to me—I mean, the sheer size is amazing, no?'

While the guides continued to educate the 'interested' trip members about the importance of the Arch, Kate and I walked around the bus, trying to get away from the minders as much as possible, sneaking in pictures of the landscape and locals with lapel pins bent over the grassy sidewalk. No one looked up at us.

The first few hours were crucial for relationship-building and it was absolutely important not to irk the guides if we intended to enjoy the rest of the trip. But really we didn't have to worry that much—Miss Deer, Giraffe and Li were really friendly and didn't object to our unauthorised pictures at the Arch. Clearly, we were being watched.

That was good to know.

As we drove through the city, things got easier inside the bus.

The enormous silhouette of a pyramid-shaped hotel loomed in the background. Come to think of it, it was visible from everywhere, an ominous ghostly presence watching over the city. However, I'd seen pictures of it on Google when looking up Pyongyang, like most of the others. The ghostly pyramid was the Ryugyong Hotel, DPRK's biggest embarrassment. I'd read reports that constantly alluded to it as the Hotel of Doom, A Colossal Engineering Failure and Ghost Hotel, all of which described it right. Apparently, the government ran out of money before the completion, so it continues to stand there, like a forgotten shell of something that could have been.

I tried to ask Miss Deer about it, but she cleverly avoided the question. Miss Deer, with all her prerequisites for being a 'Pyongyang Citizen', was clever too.

We proceeded to the Mansudae Hill to pay our respects to the Great Leader and Dear Leader. It was hard not to be impressed by the monuments seen above everything else in the city. I am not sure what we expected to find, but it wasn't this.

'You may buy flowers if you wish,' the guide called out. 'It is not compulsory, but they will definitely appreciate it.'

Then he proceeded to fix his tie, bought a bunch of flowers and walked stiffly uphill to pay the mandatory respects to the Great Leader and Dear Leader.

I didn't buy any. Neither did Kate or Larry.

'Who is "they"? Is someone watching?' This was a question I asked someone beside me. It just happened that the said someone had been thinking the exact same thing.

'You never know. They probably are. Never mind though, a few flowers may not be missed.'

At this point the surprisingly agile Mr Videoman sprang in front of us and pointing the camera got to work without giving us any time to fix a smile.

'We might end up on State TV eventually,' someone joked. 'Smile, here are your fifteen seconds of fame.'

All of us smiled and waved—only just. At the monuments, crying, not laughing, was appreciated.

The flower-bearing locals politely stepped away from the camera, turned their heads and plodded up the hill solemnly in absolute indifference to everything around. One would think visiting the Great Leader and Dear Leader was a joyous occasion, something to smile about.

Giraffe marched us to the statue and signalled for us to form a straight line.

'We will now bow to the Great Leaders. This is a one-time-bow. Then we offer the flowers. Please, no laughing or shouting here.'

Mr Videoman had his camera in place. Moments like this were precious in DPRK. Footage of tourists bowing at the statues makes it to prime time television and telecast till a new set of tourists arrived in the country. This was a ploy to impress the locals about the greatness of their country, the proof of which was the thousands of tourists who arrived from faraway lands to pay respects to their Great Leader. It helped that the tourists bowed at the feet of the Great Leader and smiled in awe at the sheer size of the monuments, that was originally gold plated but had been removed due to China's insistence. There was perhaps a reason why there were no real close-ups, but for the moment, I will let that pass.

As if on cue, everyone bowed—some stiffly, some with mock respect and me, watching the rest of the group go through the motions and hoping Mr Videoman would direct the camera away from me. I was not going to make it on TV.

I have seen big statues and monuments. It is really hard to impress an Indian with a statue or a monument of any size. We are a country full of such things. Give us a rock or wood and we will carve a statue and dedicate it to one of the thousand gods watching over us. But even to my monument-hating mind, this was humbling. The figures were so lifelike, so ethereal. So human. It was eerie.

Here, from awe to tears, you could see pretty much everything and whatever you saw was genuine, even the frustration and anger that appeared on the visitors' faces.

I wandered away from the group when Giraffe launched into a passionate explanation of Korean history pointing at the reliefs carved into marble. He had a tendency to start with the defeat of Americans before going on to fictionalise and glorify the great power of the Great Leader Kim Il Sung who single-handedly thwarted the Japanese to secure freedom for Korea. Few listened with interest, others pretended, but everyone was a part of the audience watching a stage play.

And suddenly, as if to add to the drama, it started to rain. Just like that.

It was a typical Bollywood setting—grey clouds, gently falling rain, smiling statues, mountain of flowers, happy and curious visitors…and in such a Bollywood-type setting, the thing to do is dance. Because in Bollywood, rains make an appearance in two extreme cases—one, when you are full of joy and want to dance and two, when you are invoking a deity and start to dance.

I was full of joy. And I wanted to dance. Well, I really mean swirl, smile and throw my arms about, to inject a little drama into this make-believe setting so devoid of life and colour. Bollywood style. I think it was when I put away my camera lenses and was going to throw my arms about, Mr Videoman held up an umbrella and I had no choice but follow him back to the bus in silence.

ജ്ജ

A number of unfinished buildings dotted the city, waiting for time to breathe life into it. Pyongyang was like a Potemkin Village built on an enormous scale to dazzle the few tourists permitted to visit the country. It was a city that looked great in photographs—with its uniform rows of drab grey apartment blocks, monuments and impressive façades. A city of wide, clean streets, beautiful monuments and grand public buildings.

What it did not have was people. And life. And colour. Traffic jam. Noise. It was missing something essential called—People.

But you have to give it to the Koreans or the Regime to be precise—they had mastered the art of creating an entire city for impression's sake but then the North Koreans thrived on creating impressions of greatness. Even in their madness, there was a method. A motive. But if you looked carefully enough, meaning, if you had great camera lens and zoomed in close, you could notice the absence of glass on the windows or electric bulbs or people in those drab apartment blocks. Period. Pyongyang was more like a city built to be seen and toured, not lived in.

There was a strange unreality about it. Unfortunately what we were seeing was real. DPRK was a real country.

During our first meal, along with the rice cakes, duck, chicken, fish, potatoes, cold noodles, salads and soups, I made my first contact with the Kimchi. I might add here that looking at the sheer unnecessary spread quelled any fear about going hungry on the trip.

The kimchi, Korea's national dish was essentially fermented cabbage and spiced up according to taste. I like cabbage, mind you. I really do, but not kimchi.

While we dined, the guides had disappeared. When I called for Miss Deer to enquire about buying a silver chopstick like the one I was eating with, she appeared from somewhere else.

Kate whispered, 'I thought she was eating with us?'

Chopsticks forgotten, the first thing I asked was, 'Why aren't you eating with us? There is some much food here, join us?'

Miss Deer looked embarrassed and a little sad, 'No, we eat inside.'

Only later I learnt that the guides, minders or whoever else accompanied us on the trip were bound by rules—the tourists indulged in the best DPRK had to offer, the locals ate rice with kimchi.

It was a requirement of the regime. A communist philosophy.

I had known this about North Korea, I guess pretty much everyone else did too. DPRK was in the grip of a severe famine and thus their diet remained insufficient and inadequate—restricted mostly to cabbage and rice provided by the government. Cabbage was spiced up to add life to an otherwise bland meal. The only exception to this food was the occasional cold noodles, cucumber salad or potatoes, and the yearly quota of pork, fish and butter.

I think at this point, I began to hate kimchi altogether.

Our first night at Changgwangsan Hotel, Kate asked me a question. I knew we would be friends for life.

'Let's check if the room is bugged.'

I loved the girl. She had the kind of romantic spirit that makes even a bleak and bare hotel room in DPRK seem interesting and important. It was the way she spoke that took the edge off a reality we faced.

We were not good at it, but we searched the room as quietly and thoroughly as possible, including the lampshade and curtain folds and inside the kettle. Satisfied with the results of our amateur search, she asked me another question.

'Say, you aren't a school teacher, are you? You don't look it, you know.'

Thus Kate became the first person on the trip to know the truth about me. I didn't even ask her what gave me away. When I told her the whole story, she was excited.

'You know, I write also. I like to write.'

Kate, it turned out, was also a published author and lived in constant fear that her Polish book about China might get translated into Mandarin and all hell would break loose.

'I am a translator, you know, Chinese translator, so I don't want to lock horns with China.'

The more she told me about herself, the more I liked her. Kate had lived in Taiwan for a year before moving to China for two years to do her PhD in Social Sciences, spoke fluent Chinese, loved travelling and had a great sense of humour.

And humour we definitely needed to get through our short and expensive trip to North Korea.

We stepped out on the unfinished, dusty balcony to face sheer darkness around broken only by a few flickering street lights. The drab concrete structures lining the streets were dark.

'It looks spooky, eerie. Like a big ghost town…'

That gap, between two worlds, one of the visitors and the other real one for the locals, had become even more noticeable after sunset. While we sat in a well-lit restaurant for dinner, the city outside turned pitch-black.

North Korea has acute shortage of electricity and the showpiece capital city is not an exception, which means apartment dwellers often trudged up the stairs to their homes and shivered in the harsh winters for lack of heating. There were hardly any street lights, the headlights of the few passing cars lit up a small patch of the black road—enough to cast long twisting shadows among the crowds of people returning home from work. The grey apartment blocks became black shapes that loomed like barren mountains in the background. Only a few isolated pinpricks of lights—perhaps one or two windows in a vast apartment block—gave any indication of the life within. It was hard to believe we were in the middle of DPRK's capital city.

We slept badly that night.

The route to the demilitarised zone, the DMZ, took us through the Reunification Highway where we had our first glimpse of the countryside. DMZ was the highlight of the trip—naturally, we were going to visit the world's most heavily guarded border. Fancy that.

Earlier that morning while waiting for the group to finish breakfast, I had innocently crossed the street in front of the hotel, half expecting someone to appear with a gun or handcuffs or both, but nothing happened. But in stepping out of line, I felt a strange sense of freedom. I don't know what it was about defying a simple rule that made me feel alive—I felt alive.

On board the bus however, everyone in the group thought it fit to remind me of the rules.

'No wandering away from the group.'

'You could get arrested.'

'It's for your own safety'—this of course was meant to mock the rule.

Mr Videoman got into the seat behind me and Li-the-minder sat on the seat across. I swear from there on, Mr Videoman kept his camera fixed on me. I am not sure if he was recording anything, but he made it look like he was. Even on the moving bus.

I gave him a chocolate bar to soften him a little.

When we stopped at a rest area straddling the empty highway, he offered to take my pictures. He was surprisingly good too, turning the surrounding fields of corn, green hillocks and happy bunch of tourists buying t-shirts and propaganda posters into perfect postcard pictures. I couldn't help but wish he was elsewhere making something of his talent.

I didn't know how to convey this thought to him either.

I relaxed a little when I realised that my being followed around had something to do with being Indian, who were few or non-existent on group tours into North Korea.

Miss Deer walked up to me during our first break. I was surprised, but her curiosity was infectious.

'We do not see many Indian tourists,' she said to me. 'India is very beautiful, correct? I think it's very nice. You came from India?'

'Uh, yes. New Delhi.' It was a lie, of course. But there was a good chance she had heard of New Delhi.

'You are Hindu, correct?'

I nodded. It didn't matter.

'Once I met one Indian man. He was very nice. Always smiling. Indians always smile, yes?'

I could have told her stories about India but I also had to convince her that I had come to Korea out of genuine interest and was hoping to learn more from her. Don't get me wrong, all of them were convinced socialists and wouldn't even think of criticising the system—but they didn't try to impose their views on us and they were very interested in what we had to say, which was really commendable. Her English was perfect, despite never having travelled abroad and we spoke a lot. I don't know how much of it was true, but Miss Deer was truthful about one thing—she wanted to visit China someday.

When we finally arrived at the entrance to the DMZ, there was a brief stop at the parking lot where we had to get off the bus, listen to an officer who briefed us about the layout of DMZ, then lined up, army style and watched over by tall soldiers with automatic rifles as we marched through a gate to board the bus again.

And it was hot.

Here I might add that when we were being lined up, Miss Deer and Giraffe constantly pleaded with us not to get out of line or take photographs.

Not taking photographs was okay—I mean, the place was full of men in uniforms and spy cameras on trees, rooftops and walls. But what Miss Deer said after this shocked us.

'Do not laugh very loudly here, okay? For your own safety.'

'Will they shoot us?' That was me.

'Yes.'

We marched through the gate in a single line, feigning solemnity, trying to humour Ms Deer.

'Oh, I want to laugh so hard you know,' Kate whispered. 'But I will not—for my own safety. You know, this is like some horror movie. Look at those concrete blocks? I think it is to thwart enemies if they crossed here.'

'Shhhh, girl.'

The blocks were indeed rigged with cables to fall and block the path entirely in the event of an attack. But despite all this DMZ was a surprisingly peaceful place. Quiet. There were no people other than the men in uniform.

I waited till we re-boarded to offer my own opinion.

'I am sure they must be very bored with cleaning their guns without the chance of ever shooting anyone. I guess they want us to laugh so they could shoot us,' is what I said.

We were led through a building where the armistice had been signed in 1953. It was of course historically interesting but uneventful. The real border was still some distance away. I did not see a reason not to hurry straight to the border because nothing else made any sense to me. Ours was a large group and everything was lost in translation although much of the story remained DPRK-centric. They somehow managed to give an impression that the world and everything in it was made up of DPRK (the victim) and America (the tormentor) and the saviour of the world—The Great Leader who had made the impossible, possible.

But we eventually arrived at the border.

Directly opposite the marbled, futuristic-looking building we were standing on, was a similar building which at the moment was empty.

'That is South Korea,' Giraffe pointed out not too happily. 'You see that line? Yes, that separates us. But one day we hope there will be no borders.'

Between the two enemy countries was a series of bright blue huts where the army officers of U.S.A., South Korea and North Korea met regularly to discuss practical issues related to maintaining the ceasefire. In the gap between each hut was a thin concrete line, about a foot across, which marked the final boundary separating each side's territory.

I asked Giraffe an innocent question.

'What if one of us ran across the line?'

'You'll be shot,' he said.

An answer like that does not leave room for further conversation so I busied myself with the pictures.

We entered one of the blue huts and took seats around the tables inside. I was on the far side, on the South Korean side as informed by the guides. In the excitement of taking a memorable picture 'between the enemy lines' I did not pay attention to the exact number of times Americans breached the armistice. I vaguely remember eighty-eight thousand times, but I could have been mistaken.

I loved my first time on South Korean soil. Let's leave it at that.

Safely back on the soil of Fatherland—meaning not being gunned down by the enemies or American snipers employed just for the purpose—Giraffe told us another story, a little more fantastic one this time. He was a true loyalist, he was and as he rattled off a story about Kim Jong-Il's visit to Panmunjom, his expressions changed. He looked like a maverick magician ready to perform the ultimate trick.

Larry was about to explode.

'I don't believe he ever actually went there. Why would he have put himself in the enemy's firing line?' Larry whispered.

Unmindful of hurting the sentiments of Imperialist Bastards (aka, the Americans), Giraffe continued to enlighten us with his tale.

'When the Dear Leader was inspecting this site, a cloud of smoke came down and covered the place so his enemies could not see him. But,' here he paused importantly, 'but, the Great Leader could easily see the other side. The enemy could not. He easily inspected the site and left unharmed.'

In North Korea, you had to believe a story like that. As long as there was a Great Leader or a Dear Leader as the protagonist of the story, everything was possible. For example, with one of the Kims at the helm, you could call the shots with the winds and heavens at the very least. Smokescreens were just, by-the-way.

Why, you could even rewrite history!

Our next stop was a visit to an old, restored and beautiful Confucian temple that somehow escaped destruction. It doubled up as a museum. It was beautiful, yes, but at that moment I couldn't have cared less. I was tired. I think everyone was—with the exception of the know-it-all Norwegian who was at the head of all queues.

The compound was completely enclosed, and I couldn't have been too far from the group but suddenly Li-the-minder appeared from nowhere and gestured me to join the others.

'Stay with the group!' he half ordered, half pleaded. 'For your own safety.'

I had heard that before. It had started to get on my nerves.

We plodded along in our sweat-soaked misery, while the guides continued in all sincerity to drill the goodness of Korea into us. Giraffe looked so sincere, despite the sweat running down his face. Mr Videoman tirelessly lugged his camera around, Li-the-minder continued looking serious and unsmiling, and Miss Deer, poor Miss Deer with her shiny hair stuck to her face, carried on bravely, not losing the sweetness in her voice.

They worked hard, they did. They had no choice. We were on their land yet, they were the prisoners of their regime. Everything had to be perfect. Every story had to be true; for this, they had to believe in it first, even if they thought otherwise. I don't know if they thought otherwise, but they had no doubts about the strength of their Great Leader. One would think their interactions with the tourists would have somehow opened their minds about the truth of their regime, at least a little, but one couldn't be sure.

I drifted back to the bus. I was tired.

We broke for lunch in Kaesong, the city closest to DMZ and home to a big industrial park where South Korean companies have been allowed to set up cross-border factories, which sadly was not on our itinerary. It was cloudy and humid. I hoped it would rain. I followed along at the tail end of our group, dragging my heels alongside an equally deflated group member sweating buckets and muttering under his breath. I was sick to the gills of monuments, propaganda and especially stories about the Leader and I think I can safely assume eighty-five per cent of the members fell under this category.

We were not done. There was more evidence of the North Korean greatness to be seen and understood and the Revolutionary Martyr's Cemetery was one such place where we were directed to expand our knowledge of the Korean War against Japan. Under the skies steadily turning dangerous grey, we trudged up the hill and continued walking past a sea of lifelike busts of brave people who lost their lives securing freedom for their country. To me everyone looked the same but you could put that down to poor lighting.

Nothing wipes off your cheer faster than moping about communist monuments in North Korea. I mean, there was only so much yarn you could listen to or see all those god-awful militant revolutionary monuments. I drifted.

Besides, I was more interested in the far-off view of the Pyongyang cityscape, with its enormous pyramid hotel that towered over everything. That strange black pyramid—that heartless shell—would begin to show up in more and more of my photographs. It mesmerised me. It lured me in. It was slowly becoming an obsession.

Why do they need so many large hotels when they don't allow tourists? Perhaps the Great Leader was planning ahead for the tourist boom to come? That would explain the ten-lane highways as well, currently without any traffic.

At the top of the hill was a surprise—the grave of Kim Jong-Il's mother, who, according to the recent version of history was also a revolutionary hero. Locals had lined up to pay their respects, some wept real tears; a bunch of school children gave us curious looks and went back to adding their share of flowers to an already swelling mountain of flowers at her feet.

And while we lined up to perform the mandatory 'one-time-bow'—just one of the prices we paid for being here—it started to rain.

I succumbed to the moment.

I whooped in joy. Spreading out my arms, I swirled before realising that I had become the focus of scorn and hate. If anything was likely to get me arrested, it was this—but at that moment I couldn't have cared less.

It was improper to dance at a cemetery, of course, but it was also blissful. It was worth being arrested for, if I might add. Kate, bless her, somehow managed to snap me doing just that. So I have a picture to prove my claim. To a newbie, I would appear to have a knack for finding and keeping self-incriminating evidence, but to anyone who has been in DPRK, such moments really work in your favour if you manage to return in one piece and are narrating the story around a campfire.

I just wanted to feel alive. To let the rains wash down the sweat and the lies of North Korea.

That night we stayed at Yanggakdo, DPRK's four star-rated hotel. But it didn't happen just like that. Like everything else, there was a lot of drama about a simple act of moving into a new hotel.

We were returning from the various monument-visits when suddenly Miss Deer picked up the mike and announced.

'Today we will stay at the best hotel in Korea. Yes, today we will stay at Yanggakdo Hotel. We have been upgraded.'

We cheered.

After this, our tour coordinator from Beijing grabbed the mike and seconded what Miss Deer had just said—although with a little more animosity. He threw up his arms and did a little jig on the moving bus and stressed how beautiful the view from the top was. He was British.

'There is also lots of beer.'

We cheered again.

No one however explained how the upgrade came about or why.

We couldn't have kidded ourselves that the regime had taken a shine to us and set us up in this grand island hotel—but you never know. It could have been just that—or it was just easy to watch over a group after isolating them from the rest of the world without leaving any chance of escape.

But at least it was a good hotel. Or so we had been told.

Miss Deer then decided to entertain us with a song. She clearly was the happiest to be staying with us at Yanggakdo Hotel.

She began with a story though.

Like every folklore in the world her story too started with two lovers and ended tragically with the man leaving his beloved over a misunderstanding. The misunderstood woman with a broken heart watched the retreating back of her lover and leaned over the window and called out to the valley below. The lovely valleys then echoed piteous pleas for her lover to return. Thus the song was born.

Her voice was as beautiful as she was. Her heart was in every word of the song that played on her lips and even without the music it was beautiful. I had the good sense to record it, but that is besides the point right now.

That song was *Aarirang.*

We arrived at the hotel.

Hotel Yanggakdo was impressive. And secluded. It stood all by itself on an island in the Taedong river which divides the city. Perfect place to keep the foreign tourists, away from trouble they were likely to cause if allowed to come in contact with the locals. It was another thing that the government wanted our money, but it was against their principles to allow us freedom to walk the streets on our own. North Korea was contradictory like that.

There was also a lone turtle in the hotel and a small store, besides the mandatory giant pictures of the Kims. It was self-contained if you wanted to include the casino and the golf course too. Hotel Yanggakdo was special in many ways. If you didn't mind someone listening in to your phone conversation that cost you USD 6 a minute, then you were welcome to use the facility. Before you jump the gun, remember that it was the only place in the whole of Pyongyang where you could do that. The trick was to speak in a tongue you hoped the spies couldn't interpret.

I tried Hindi. I could have given Arabic a shot too—but I simply had to connect with someone outside. I called Nitin, who was currently in Canada. I admit to crying a little when I heard his voice, but the thought of paying a few hundred dollars if I kept that up dried my tears quickly. I wanted to leave. Just leave. Go to Canada, Dubai or Timbuktu…anywhere but away from here.

Unconsciously, the pressure of being here was dragging me down—or it could have been my mind playing tricks, forcing me to feel strongly because, let's face it, we were tuned to think that way.

I was tired.

The moment passed. Kate, who had been hovering about the telephone booth, looked excited.

'There is a casino somewhere, let's go check it out.'

Then seeing my unhappy expression—'Are you crying? I mean you? But why?'

I had no answer to that and I felt like a complete idiot so I decided to give in to her casino idea.

We set out.

Here, I beg to digress. I am a big fan of the movie *Casablanca*. I am equally or more fond of the song of the same name. I dream of visiting Rick's Candlelit Café in Morocco one day soon. But somehow, here in Yanggakdo, looking at the hotel lobby, I felt as though I was living the Casablanca dream. The lobby was sort of a meeting point for people—tourists, diplomats, aid workers, businessmen, mainly Chinese. Here for a moment you could forget that you were being watched, at least briefly, and let your hair down at the bar. Here, the guides also became human. Over beers, they happily chatted about their families and education and tried to understand lives outside Korea.

The rooms in Yanggakdo were basic yet comfortable but the view made up for it. We were on the thirty-second floor but it was possible to fully open the windows, just in case you wanted to jump out and escape that way. I am not complaining, mind, for I have stayed in far worse places. I am a backpacker, for the love of God, so an occasional mosquito or a bed bug was right up my alley. DPRK did have some redeeming qualities—this hotel also had a few good comments on Tripadvisor which says a lot.

And there was a TV. And BBC.

Kate and I went down to the casino, only to notice that the lifts did not stop on the fifth floor. We didn't make too much of it, until someone else brought it up with Giraffe over dinner.

I will freely admit that it was like walking back in time. It was weird. Not a James Bond-style casino this, it was more like the Crouching Tiger Hidden Dragon-style something from ancient China, and while I am not an authority on casinos, the absence of life and pulse here bothered me somehow. It was also musty and like everything else, old and spooky. We retired for dinner.

Over dinner when the question of the fifth floor came up, Giraffe's transformation from a happy-go-lucky guide to a stern-faced patriot was swift. He at once became curt and businesslike and muttered under his breath, trying to slip away without offering an explanation.

Fortunately, no one pressed the question but an uneasy feeling had crept in. I felt as though time had stopped. Even the night passed in slow motion. I was never in such a hurry to see sunlight.

For the second night, we slept badly.

As I stood by the window peering into the black river below, I wondered about North Korea, a country so full of contradictions. It is a surprise that the system has survived for so long. How could a few thousand tourists really make a difference?

By morning, I had no answers.

I started to wonder why North Korea even allows those tourists, because it didn't really make sense. Yes, a few thousand dollars came into the country but was that the real reason? I don't think it's about the money, because there are not nearly enough tourists visiting the DPRK to justify the effort. In Pyongyang I could see it was about changing foreigners' minds or creating a positive image of a country in the outside world. And again, did they really care that much?

THE SLOW TRAIN TO BEIJING

The morning was grey, like a grand setting for the sombre event we were about to embark upon—a visit to the Mausoleum, Kumsusan Palace of the Sun.

In North Korea, it was a big deal.

The tour coordinators had stressed the need to wear pants, shirts and tie during the briefing in Beijing and again at the earlier evening dinner. I suppose, if you were going to a mausoleum to see bodies of two of the greatest men that walked the earth, it was absolutely necessary to wear a tie and a shirt. Just being prim and proper, but that's all.

The men in the group, true to norm arrived in shirts, pants and ties. Valerie, hitherto seen only in shorts, had put on pants, same as I, while Kate looked fabulous in a blue dress. There was much joy despite the solemnity of the upcoming visit, but we were a happy bunch like that. No tomb was going to dampen our spirits, least of all Kate's because she was particularly chirpy over breakfast, excited at finding thin rice porridge such as she'd loved in China. After that, there was no stopping her.

Miss Deer, Giraffe, Li-the-minder and Mr Videoman were unsmiling and businesslike as though leading us to our execution but not quite sure how to tell us about it.

When we left for the tombs, it started to rain.

The mausoleum of Kim Il-Sung, DPRK's founder and his son Kim Jong-Il, is the most sacred spot in all of DPRK, same as the Vatican or Mecca or Thirupathi or perhaps all of them put together and given its divine status, it was necessary to observe proper courtesies. Nothing could go wrong here. The slightest lapse could lead to grave consequences. Arrest and deportation, but you know that about DPRK already.

Koreans in general undertake this holy pilgrimage at least twice a year as part of the required duty of their work unit. To see the Great Leader, a virtual god among men, the epitome of human perfection in all respects defines their afterlife. The occasion was of National Importance and it was the birthright of every Korean to be allowed to visit the tomb, although they had to get the permission of their work units first.

We arrived at the grand monument. Miss Deer picked up the mike.

'This is the largest and the grandest mausoleum ever built for a Communist Leader. This was once upon a time Kim Il-Sung's official residence.'

We entered the hallowed hallway. Kate, Larry and I formed our own little sub-group and stayed at the back of the line.

'At the time this fantastic mausoleum was being rebuilt, thousands were starving to death here,' Larry explained to us. 'I wonder why all this.'

Through the marbled corridors we marched steadily and grimly, as the occasion demanded. Outside the rains had filled up the moats surrounding Kumsusan turning it into a ridiculously large pool of fresh water, cutting out every chance of escape that way.

It was a little spooky all right, but it could have been just the weather.

Then the security checks began.

The cameras went first, followed by the wallets and just about everything else that was in our pockets. Nothing could be taken into the sacred interiors. Not even an SD card but that was a given because cameras were strictly not allowed—they were very pedantic like that. Considering the given situation, it is unnecessary to add that photography was impossible under the circumstances. So, all I have brought back from the visit are the mental pictures of the bodies of the Great Leaders lying in eternal sleep.

But I will come to that later.

Briefly I shall tell you what to do in case you find yourself here. Once past the security gate, observe complete silence all the time. No hushed discussions, no smiles, no furtive or meaningful glances at each other. Keep pace with the guides, show proper respect towards the thousands of pictures hanging on the walls as you walk through ridiculously long hallways to descend into the bowels of the earth.

Once you have reached deep inside the marbled earth, step on to a series of moving walkways that would put Dubai International Airport to shame. Remember that the length of the walkway is several kilometres, pardon me if I exaggerate, and you must not walk on them. You are required to stand on it and let yourself be carried along. But in those painfully long minutes, you see the make-believe world of peace and contentment in North Korea in the thousands of framed photographs adorning the walls, each picture outdoing the other in terms of greatness. Every face in those pictures is happy, every frame itself reflecting deemed prosperity—and not for a moment can you allow yourself to think that DPRK is one of the poorest countries in the world.

Such is the opulence of the palace.

At the end of this long journey is a marble foyer. Here you line up and march forward, army-style, with hands on your side, into another hall where a pure white marble statue of Kim Il-Sung towers over you. It is hard not to get carried away by the grandeur. I mean, yes, I have seen Taj Mahal, but this was something else.

It also reduces you to tears. On a screen behind the great marble statue is a warm pink glow of sunrise below a clear blue sky. You can interpret it anyway you want, but the guide will tell you that in Korea, the sun always rose with the Kims.

It was beautiful, yes, but it was also eerie. Unreal. You might get the feeling that time has stopped. Somehow.

After this visual overkill, you march down a hall through a narrow doorway that blows air at passersby. This of course is meant to remove every speck of dust and dirt from your mortal bodies. Only when you have passed this cleaning ritual, can you enter the next hall.

Here on, things get bizarre.

In a vast, glowing red chamber, Kim Il-Sung lay peacefully asleep inside a glass sarcophagus.

The Red Chamber buzzes with energy that is as emotional as it is real—easily the first real thing you will see in DPRK. Groups of local women in *hanbok,* the traditional Korean dress worn by women, silently shed tears. Men try hard not to, while soldiers on their mandatory visit know exactly when to bow, where to look and how to behave.

We formed three rows. At a slight nod, we walked respectfully ahead, with hands at our sides, one step at a time towards the open casket, lined up again and waited for the signal to bow.

Here it is mandatory to bow thrice and as soon as you are done, you are required to leave the hall. Much as you'd like to stare or take in all this bizarreness, you may not do so. But if you are a quick observer, you'd notice armed guards strategically installed behind pillars watching your moves. Any sign of trouble, namely the slightest change of expression from anguish to joy or relief is quickly noticed. And perhaps punished.

The same procedure is repeated for Kim Jong-Il in another chamber, by which time your senses are numb. It takes a while to breathe normally again and when that happens you wonder when had you stopped breathing altogether.

We returned the way we'd come; only this time, no one had anything to say, not even Larry or Kate. Each of us was lost somewhere—inside the Red Chamber perhaps, because only the absurdity of the Red Chamber could shock us into silence. The tension snapped as we arrived at our buses. The rains had stopped and we were chattering openly with each other, barely noticing the endless parade of hostile stares from North Koreans passing us on their way in.

Outside, the locals returning from their visit to the tombs were laughing and waving, a strange behaviour indeed, like holiday-makers out strolling in their Sunday best. No longer in the immediate presence of the Great Leader, the tension had suddenly dissipated for them as well, and they had resumed their role as regular human beings. It was one of the precious few chances we had to interact with everyday North Koreans in a relatively unconstrained setting. But we had to leave.

I have my own reasons to omit details of our visit to some other places, such as the visit to the Victorious Fatherland Liberation War Museum which had Larry and Valerie in knots, a tour of the captured American ship, the bookstore that sold only books on the Great Leaders and Juche Philosophy, the fake Tiananmen-like Square, the bowling alley with no electricity, the tram ride around the city, and the elevator ride to the Juche Tower, which I cleverly avoided by staying on in the bus, pretending to be sick.

The reason for this was a remote chance of dashing to the local pub we had earlier visited without supervision. Of course, I was not alone, for Miss Deer volunteered to stay with me but without the pressure of a large group to mind, she was relaxed enough to talk and let me take pictures as I pleased.

I had once read something about DPRK being '10% researched and 90% fictionalised'. It was true. I have, on many occasions, wanted to fling stuff at the guides for their endless, meaningless yarn, but that's the truth of North Korea I had come to see. There was no reason for me to get upset or knotted up on the subject of their philosophy or political leanings.

Pyongsung, DPRK's University City came as a relief, a welcome escape from the fake glamour and the monuments of Pyongyang. I have never been in any hotel that made me think of ghosts so much as this hotel in Pyongsung did. Everything was so large and so empty—so ghoulish—and the smell of mouldy carpets and curtains was strong enough to knock you out. The good thing about this old hotel was that it was hard to bug it and on that note, after a cold dinner followed by a power cut, Kate and I slept peacefully that night.

Things had improved considerably the next morning. I suppose a good night's sleep was the reason, so Pyongsung's only monument was a welcome sight where we spent considerable time photographing the passable reality, but in hindsight, it was better than what followed next.

We went to a school.

It is universally known that The Kims love children. No photograph is complete without a bunch of happy bounders surrounding a Kim. No one explained this obsession with happy children, but children, it appeared, were clearly much loved.

I have reasons to shudder at this part of the trip and I am about to give you a reason.

To a school we went. It was surprisingly a very quiet and well-behaved school—no sound of running feet, no groups of girls whispering in corners, no boys sliding down railings. It was silent. If we hadn't been talking to each other or breathing, perhaps we could hear pins drop.

But it was a school all right, with real children in uniforms and teachers with the proper 'teacher-face'. If it was meant to deceive us, well, then clearly the elaborate deception worked.

The classrooms were real too. As real as one could expect a school room in DPRK to be with prim and proper unsmiling students facing stern-faced teachers, dwarfed by the mandatory picture of the Kims.

We broke into the class for a 'pre-arranged' lecture by the tourists; students shifted their expressions to resemble a smile and teachers respectfully stood aside to let the foreign tourists help the beloved students brush up their English-speaking skills.

Okay, so it did not matter that of the lot of 'lecturing tourists' there were a few imperialist bastards, namely the Americans and that included Larry, because the principles of Juche were accommodating that way—American tutors were all right, as were the dollars. The enmity lay in the Americans' failure to recognise Korean supremacy.

Giraffe sidled up to me.

'Your turn next. You are a teacher. I am sure you will enjoy this very much. Our children are very bright. First time they will learn from an Indian teacher. Come on, next. Please.'

That shook me up. As I have said before, I couldn't convince a child to sing a nursery rhyme, let alone interest a bunch of high school students with travel talk. I'd never taught a class and it didn't help that the children looked scary in their stiff uniforms. I also didn't look the part, which was really the bummer. I am not sure if I was ever embarrassed by a group of eager kids staring at my legs, but clearly if I went up on that podium, it would be my first.

If I did muster the courage to give a short lecture, I would give myself away. I'd be a sitting duck—and that I wasn't going to have. We still had another day in DPRK and the risk of blowing my cover was high. It would even jeopardise the tour company that had brought me in.

I thought quickly.

'Oh no…I have had enough of kids to be honest, and, phew, I am glad to be on a break and not have to teach them. So, no, I will pass. Thanks for the offer though.'

Giraffe didn't understand. He persisted.

'Really, you must. First time our children have an Indian teacher. Please.'

'Nope. I rather want to feel as though I am on a holiday, you see? Teaching will make it feel like work!'

I swear I saw Larry give me a curious look. Kate was nowhere to be seen. And before Giraffe could say something, I slipped out of the room and into the bathroom, which was surprisingly unused and empty.

Giraffe may have begun to suspect something then, but I had left the scene and hence missed, as Kate told me later, a tour of the children's playroom that consisted entirely of stuffed animals and paintings made by the children depicting gruesome deaths of American soldiers at the hands of Korean loyalists.

'You should have spoken to the kids, you know,' she winked. 'I am sure you would be good at it, you know. Tell them about your travels.'

I shuddered. I had to be on my guard till I left DPRK for good and suddenly the hours seemed one too many. Or perhaps given my nervous state every apparent danger in DPRK seemed so big and out of proportion? I couldn't tell.

Back on the bus heading to a clothing factory, my tour coordinator whispered hushed warnings in my ear asking me to watch out for Li-the-minder who was good at sniffing out a rat anywhere.

After this we became the first ever tourist group to visit the Pyongsong Taedonggang Clothing Factory. The factory has been in operation since 1961 when it used to manufacture work clothes for export to Russia and later to Vietnam, then baby clothes to Japan and currently, they were employed in manufacturing ski-wear for the popular brand Ripcurl. This was what real people did. These workers who created things with their own hands were real. The yards of clothes that went through the sewing machines were real.

That could not be faked, like the school.

There was a strange realism about the factory women in their multicoloured uniforms, bent over their aging machines under slow-moving fans, stitching materials for a brand which would eventually carry a 'Made in China' label and be sold at an exorbitant price in a shopping mall somewhere.

But here, amidst the humming of machines, there was no extolling the greatness of Korea. That moment when they went about their work took away the severity of the situation I was in.

These women formed an important part of the working society that kept the economic mills running, yet to see them like that was painful. They were so oblivious, so unquestioning, so involved in their work, toiling hard—only to receive food coupons or a very meagre salary at the end of a long hard month of labour. I am not sure if I would ever wear a Ripcurl brand again knowing where it had come from. I had felt the same about Vietnam long ago.

I asked Giraffe what the women received in return.

'Free food, free house, free medicine and free education. Here in Korea, everything is free. The Great Leader provides everything.'

That put an end to every other question I wanted to ask. He was not forthcoming; probably miffed at my refusal to teach the kids, but I didn't want to find out. I withdrew.

I was also tired. I missed home. I missed Nitin. It was probably all that kimchi. Or the hotpot. Or even the darned monuments, the fear, or a combination of everything, but it had taken a toll.

I wanted fruit juice, I wanted real coffee. None was to be had. Pyongsung was an old town really. Dilapidated buildings and rutted roads made it look as though it was in an advanced state of decay. It kind of dipped our spirits and I think I was glad to get back to Pyongyang, despite the monuments. I constantly thought about the long train ride back to Beijing. I wanted to be on that train as soon as possible.

And as though reading my mind, Kate said, 'I want to get back to Pyongyang.'

Pyongyang's underground metro is an interesting piece of art. I recorded the slow descent into the earth's core—two minutes and twenty-two seconds.

I felt as though we were being taken into some secret underground bomb shelter. Well, I have never been inside a bomb shelter, but I have seen war movies, so I can make a fairly intelligent guess. But when we finally stepped on to the marble platform and were greeted by the smiling Kims under the sheer brilliance of the giant chandeliers, all doubts I had about the North Koreans disappeared.

Miss Deer and Giraffe looked particularly proud.

I learnt later that a visit to the underground metro was a standard stop on all tours, although at that time we were sure we were the first ever to be allowed to ride on it. No matter what, the subway system is fantastic. It is about forty-five years old and impressive as a replica of a Russian subway that sometimes looks like a miniature cathedral.

Glittering chandeliers hang from the white marble ceiling, while frescos of joyful Koreans cover the walls. The subway cars are rickety and old, probably from the original rolling stock. Passengers, directed by female conductors in smart blue uniforms, move on and off with a purpose. In both the stations we saw, dual portraits of Kims were present. Of course, could anything else be expected?

A map on the wall of the next station depicts a rather extensive subway network, with several stations scattered across Pyongyang. I can't say whether this is true or not, but it sounds a bit outlandish to me. It might be true that there aren't actually that many stops, and that the other stations aren't anywhere near as fancy but whatever we saw, was fancy. Eye-catching.

You have to give the Koreans that. They know how to keep their marbles polished.

Our unscheduled stop at one of the local breweries pretty much signalled the end of our tour. This was time to bond—and over Beers No. 3, 4 and 5 everyone had become friends. Some, including me and Kate, said how we would miss DPRK but I am not sure we convinced anyone, least of all Li-the-minder who had stuck to my side ever since we left the metro. But it was the thing to say—as travellers we said it all the time, we probably meant it too.

It was during this beer-drinking binge, when Li-the-minder had one too many, that I got my first chance to walk around a little. Kate stayed back to catch up with the rest of the tour members, she was not as anti-social as I was being.

No one came after me. I suppose since we were leaving the next morning and had not caused any troubles just yet, it seemed agreeable to the guides to ease surveillance. I stood by the road and watched people getting in and out of the beer parlour, people walking through the gates into their homes, people on the trams passing by.

In that hour I touched the real Korea. I saw real people. I wondered if they would ever be able to cope with the outside world, if they would ever consider another God or rule. If they would ever know the internet or BBC or CNN, iPhones or tablets, Adidas, Nike or even KFC, Starbucks or pizza. I don't think I could ever imagine what it was like living under a regime that allowed no outside contact, not even through internet. And why?

These questions, of course, did not have immediate answers but the moment was such that I wondered. If you took a random moment and framed it, life here would seem like that in any other country—people walking back home, people riding trams, buildings, trees, roads—but life in North Korea did not exist in picture frames. The reality was different. Each of these people going back home lived in constant fear. Saying a wrong word, failure to wear the lapel pin, a spying neighbour, speaking or making eye contact with a foreign tourist, everything was a threat. I shuddered slightly thinking just how much I could be endangering someone's life by merely attempting to talk to him, much as I wanted to. It was not a pretty thought.

The more you know about North Korea, the less it makes sense. That being said I am very glad that I did those trips. I had a lifetime worth of experiences, good and bad, met some extraordinary people, saw and did things I wouldn't have thought of in my wildest dreams.

I am not sure if I ever wanted to come back here, but I was glad that I did once.

That night, which was also our last, after an excellent barbeque dinner, we gathered around a TV screen to watch the handiwork of Mr Videoman. There was, however, one condition to this.

'You buy a copy if you like the video,' Giraffe told us good naturedly. 'You take back the wonderful memories of this great country.'

'For your own safety?' someone in the room quipped and the majority of the drunken ones broke into laughter. Mr Videoman looked confused and focused on attaching his video camera to the ancient TV.

The DVD was worth its weight in gold. Or diamond, whichever way you wanted to look at it. No one backed out of the deal. Heck, who in their right mind would not love to show off their North Korean sojourn, right?

The video was hilarious and amateurish and we were laughing so hard that we forgot we had very little time left in the country. Mr Videoman had made us all look like we loved being here, he showed us on our best behaviour, solemn where we needed to be and happy where the occasion demanded. It was a good round-up of the trip to DPRK. The video however cleverly avoided anything that would show the country in a bad light—meaning, no sign of the dead and decaying corners or expressionless people near the tram station.

To cheer for DPRK most of us decided to go back to the revolving restaurant for a round of beer. There was no saying if we would ever see each other again and that thought was enough to send everyone scurrying to the elevators to the revolving restaurant.

Valerie joined Kate and me a little later. It was the first time she was without Larry. They were flying out in the morning. Being Americans, it was the only way they could go. No long train rides for them. Valerie didn't seem particularly saddened by this, but I would have been, had I been American.

Finally, we were able to speak to each other without inhibition. The trip was over.

Valerie asked me what I really did. I told her. Her answer did not surprise me.

'You, I knew that about you already. I'd made an intelligent guess. Perhaps but Larry thought so too.' She said looking straight at me. 'Funny that we were right.'

And as an afterthought she added, 'By the way, you suck as a school teacher. You just don't have that in you, to carry off a charade. I think you are just so black and white. Bless you!'

Kate and I agreed, happily and without fear.

ജ

I was looking forward to the train ride. I love trains and twenty-three hours on a slow train between Pyongyang and Beijing was just the thing that made travels so fascinating and interesting. It would be like watching a film on North Korea's reality—to see, to observe without someone recording your movements, your breath. Those long hours crossing the countryside, those moments of silence…of finally not having ears burn with the stories of cranes that came to take away the soul of the Great Leader upon his death was a welcome thought.

Also there was only so much of a Potemkin Village that they could conjure up—the countryside would be real. I was looking forward to those slices of reality.

Our last few hours began with the usual morning routine, except that we headed straight to the train station instead of going sightseeing. I wish I had taken some photos outside instead of rushing inside with the flock, because the train station was one place where people looked as though they were capable of displaying emotions uninhibited.

The station itself was not quite busy, with only one platform from which trains to four different places left at different intervals.

Kate and I were on different coaches—she was getting off at Sinuiju and I was going to Beijing and onwards to Mongolia. I bid her goodbye sometime before she got off at her destination at about 3:30 pm.

I knew someday I would see her again.

The customs ritual at Sinuiju was something. It took us over two hours, in which we were not allowed to leave our cabin and during which time officers took away our passports for scrutiny while a few others went through our luggage thoroughly. It was also here that they went through pictures in your cameras, deleting what they thought was 'anti-Korean' and as such included pictures of soldiers, people cleaning streets or cutting grass, school-going children, buildings under construction, any shanty or slum you may have secretly photographed.

Those two hours were really the longest, at least to me because I had just the kind of pictures which could land me in trouble, but fortunately I had stuck the SD card inside soiled socks, a place I thought unlikely to be noticed.

I sailed through.

The train ride through the North Korea countryside had taken about five hours to cover the 160 kms, but it was as close to the reality of DPRK as you could get.

Finally, we crossed the river Yalu and into Dandong, China. The clearance at the Chinese customs was easily done.

I am no expert on North Korea and I don't claim to be so. Five days do not make an expert, I say. What I saw was the glimpse of what really was and who was to guess the reality? It seemed everyone had their own version of their country and one couldn't blame them for their beliefs. Truth be told, how were they to know otherwise? Let us not argue that they could read, watch TV or use the internet, because none of this was an option. The TV they watched was state-run and the shows they watched on it were government approved and generally consisted of messages from the Great Leader or the long dead eternal president.

I didn't realise until I got back to Beijing the constant pressure we'd been under. Always having to be careful about what we said, the awareness that we were permanently under surveillance, every conversation listened in to, and the seriousness of the North Korean guides with their relentless badgering propaganda.

As I left the station in Beijing, the tour coordinator singled me out—

'We cannot stop you from writing anything or publishing any photos you may have taken. We would of course ask you not to without our permission. But every time you have the urge to do something that would put us under the scanner remember Miss Deer's face.'

I remember Miss Deer's face all the time. I remember her voice, her smile, her laughter. I remember the look in her eyes and the hope that sprang in it. I have a recording of her song, *Aarirang*, which she sang often and with much love. Yet, I do not know what to wish for her.

When you arrive in North Korea, you might first ask yourself this. I did.

Is this really happening? Why am I here? Am I actually here?

When you leave, your questions might continue and although you may not have found all the answers to your questions, DPRK will continue to haunt you, amaze you.

Even when you are in this country, there is a strange isolated feeling because nobody can talk to you except your guides and even they tend to be pretty guarded. So you see, you observe and try to place it in the context of everything you have ever known about it prior to your visit and everything you see fits in.

The city of Pyongyang is a city of illusions. The people who live here are among the carefully controlled number chosen to live here for their looks, education, social status and usefulness while old, crippled and ugly people are banished to the countryside out of sight. That could explain the lack of normal people here or the presence of the best-looking ones, whichever way you want to look at it, particularly the capital's all-female corps of traffic police, despite the apparent lack of heavy traffic.

Restaurants in North Korea are meant basically for tourists and the upper class and serve regular food such as soups and grills, salads, noodles and beer. I know this because in all the restaurants we ate in, there was no sign of locals. Tourists who visit Pyongyang on a state-guided tour are the fortunate ones who enjoy more extravagant offerings such as barbecued lamb and duck—this is the grim reality of North Korea. For the rest, it is food from the Public Distribution System or the PDS.

The country is full of grand statues of the Great Leaders and patriots, advanced and modern mausoleums and war museums and you wonder why the regime would spend so much money on nuclear programmes while a large percentage of the population borders on starvation. Yes, you wonder. And yet you never find an answer.

Ever since my return I have not stopped answering questions about it. Some of the questions are embarrassingly basic and some are impertinent. I have answered questions about their food, appearance and beer. For some I have no answers, particularly for questions like—'Did you see the gulags? The nuclear reactors or Kim Jong-Un?' Sometimes it bothers me and sometimes it amuses me that people think it is some kind of a joke or a miracle that in five days I should have become an expert. How do I convince them what I saw was a part of a grand illusion that is North Korea?

How do I tell them their belief system is not unlike ours, that their isolation is the result of years of being wrapped up in their homegrown ideology? That talking to the locals would be endangering their lives more than mine? Besides, I am really not sure what I would tell them if I had the chance to talk.

I would definitely have liked the chance to speak with the locals or wander around the town without the watchful minders in tow. I would have liked to have a round of beer with the locals but that is simply not allowed. The reality is that I had no chance of interacting with the locals. Not just me, nobody had a chance. The extent of local interaction is limited to your minders, guide, maybe the waitress who serves the beer, but that would only be a miracle.

Satellite images of North Korea are interesting too—the country appears like an empty spot between the two shining nations of China and South Korea.

Giraffe once asked me what I thought about his country. Sensing the pride with which he asked the question, I hesitated to tell him my real thoughts. I tried to be diplomatic.

'It's beautiful,' I said taking the safe way out. 'It's green and I love the mountains and the rivers. I love your kimchi and the beautiful women.'

He swelled with pride.

'But most of all, your city is clean. I hate to say this, but India is not always so.'

For once, I was being honest.

Li, the minder of Miss Deer and Giraffe, who was until now a shadowy figure, watching and observing, joined the conversation. I don't think he ever thought of India that way. They knew about India and he wanted to know more.

As a parting shot, he said, 'Indians are beautiful.'

I don't know if that was in return for my compliment or if he really meant it, but if he was judging the whole of my country based on his impression of me, then I was definitely flattered.

Of late according to media reports, a number of locals have braved the icy cold waters and crossed into China, some perhaps sold as sex slaves too. One can only guess what would ever happen to them if they returned, but it won't be pretty.

Li was interested in China and had questions without sounding too curious.

I told him my version of China. I have travelled a lot in China as narrated in this book but I was not particularly fond of the place. However, I was not going to tell him that. Instead I chose some nice things to talk about—like their superb underground metro (Li bristled a little at this), their big airports, skyscrapers, shopping and the nightlife.

As I spoke, I realised I was finally falling in love with China, slowly but surely. I was eager to get back and see Beijing in the light of this new development.

'Someday I will go to China,' he said with a smile. I saw something in his eyes that I had not seen earlier. A new hope.

There were many things that were unnerving but well, it was a matter of bracing yourself for the worst in order to find and learn something most people can only dream of.

Before you visit North Korea, they give you an itinerary but when you begin your tour, nothing corresponds. You never know what you are going to see and when, until the very last minute or until you are on the bus or until you are actually at some place. The obvious reason is to discourage the visitor from pre-arranging a meeting time or place with anyone. I know this sounds extremely ridiculous, but well, something to this effect is also mentioned in the tour hand-guide.

For the world, North Korea is as elusive as Narnia or Atlantis and you really cannot blame them because of its fictionalised history, but from what I have seen or heard DPRK is definitely not a great place to live in. But then superficial observations over five days is not enough, unless you merge it with what you already know and see things with those notions in mind.

Do I want to go back to North Korea? Yeah. I am quite the sucker when it comes to visiting unusual places, but I am doubtful if I would ever be allowed entry. Not under the current regime.

My lasting memory about Pyongyang, though, is the total darkness that descends at night. At night when you look down from the revolving restaurant on the forty-seventh floor of Hotel Yanggakdo—there is nothing.

The entire city is swallowed up by darkness. Only the morning sun brings it to life.

BIG OVOO IS YOURS, BIG BENEFIT IS MINE

If you were willing to leave the comfort of your home to live in a developing country with the friendliest people, I'd say you were a heart person—a romantic. But as soon as you land in the prettiest and naturally landscaped airport crowned by clear blue skies, you would, whether you were a heart or a brain person, change your mind and set about making plans to live here. I wanted to live here forever but don't let that influence you in any way.

Perhaps the sight of Mongolia affected me strongly because only that morning I had arrived on the world's slowest and badly equipped train from Pyongyang to Beijing and I was anxious for some rest, visual treat and food that was not kimchi or Chinese noodles. So, forgive me if my first impressions of Mongolia were influenced by my experiences in the Democratic People's Republic of Korea in the not so distant past. My elation and relief for being in the home of wild horses, steppes, snow deserts, *gers*, blue skies and *aruul* instead of in Potemkin Village that was Pyongyang is hereby explained.

It was hard to find common ground between DPRK and Genghis Land. Let me correct myself—it is not my intention to draw comparisons between the two. No. That would be wrong. DPRK doesn't compare to anything in the world. It is different. Going from a regimented country to a sea of smiling faces was like an assault on the visual senses and the closer I got to the landing strip, the need to run out and breathe got stronger. I wanted to scream, maybe. Smile. And just breathe. And experience freedom.

To really stop complaining about lack of freedom, liberty, material and intellectual deprivation, I would strongly recommend a visit to North Korea at least once in your lifetime. That should put you in the right way of understanding basic human nature and its ability to adapt and give Stockholm Syndrome a whole new meaning.

My reason for visiting Mongolia was not to get over DPRK for when planning a trip I had little or no idea what I was going to encounter. In Mongolia, I had meant to experience space. Yes. I knew that in Mongolia you could go days without seeing another human, especially in the Gobi. Where else could you find such vastness? Well, along with finding space, I really wanted to experience Gobi Desert for reasons that will never be convincing enough—but that is not the point I am trying to make.

I fell in love with everything within sight on the way to the hostel from the airport. Such was my need to breathe free air, to embrace everything life represented, that I was ready to live here forever. Even before I met the good lady Doljmaa of SunPath Tours, who was arranging my desert tour, I knew I was right by coming here. Trust me when I say that nothing in the world can cure you of your need for space as quickly and as effectively as Mongolia.

And, I was also going to meet my Vietnamese Facebook friend Thuy Tran for the first time.

Yes, in Mongolia, unlike in the DPRK, you could pre-arrange a meeting with friends. I bring this up because I have this desperate need to get over DPRK by talking constantly about it.

I started to get over this as soon as I met Thuy and Doljmaa. They were the first real people I met since leaving DPRK.

Enough said.

ഇര

A merry bunch of people set out on the grand Gobi tour, away from the gridlocked city of Ulan Baatar. I sat beside the driver in the sturdy old Russian van packed tight with everything we would need for the trip. I had originally nursed the idea of driving the van at some point during the trip, but gave up as soon as we started. This was not just a van, this was a mean machine, the master of the Gobi and was built to withstand shocks and sudden plunges.

As soon as the journey began, I stopped thinking of North Korea by telling myself firmly that to truly enjoy the moment I had to let go.

There is no way I can describe the open space, the limitless horizons, the clear air, the space, the beauty, the feeling of being the only person on earth. Of course, I was expecting space and endless horizons but still I was not prepared for so much space, so few people and so much livestock.

The hours settled into a routine of being immersed in the passing countryside as we bounced along the earth roads criss-crossing all over. I often wished I could speak to the driver, ask questions or just talk but sadly he spoke no English and each time I made a hand gesture, he smiled, mumbled under his breath and raised the volume of his CD player.

The van had fallen silent—every member of the trip, Thuy included, fell asleep right away. It may have been the rhythm of the van, or it may have been something else, but they slept. I didn't. I was afraid if I did, I would miss something important.

I felt as though I was the only person in the world. It was a good feeling to have.

Such was the vastness of the countryside. So big, so much, so far, so huge and till the end of the horizon there were only blue skies kissing the earth erupting in a colourful fusion of wild flowers. Edelweiss grew everywhere and so did buttercups and wild geranium and to say that horses galloped among them in a big happy group is the ultimate compliment to the uniqueness of the place. We drove up the hills, through rivers, across fields filled with wildflowers. And oh, the wildflowers! I had been told it was wildflower season but I still wasn't prepared for meadows full of yellow, white, blue and purple.

If I really was the only person in the world, I would ride these horses to a far place, stand on the hill tops and fill my lungs with air, lie among the flowers and grass and sand and sing in the fresh Mongolian air…

It was a good thing I didn't get into a conversation with anyone just yet. The beginning is most important to build a relationship with the journey, because that is when you observe and assimilate thoughts without the influence of fellow travellers.

I was a little philosophical like that.

By the time we arrived at a little obscure village near Dalanzadgad we were hungry. Don't get the impression that you can walk into a restaurant and order off the menu. In Mongolian Gobi, choices are limited. Often, food is prepared against order so you might have to wait or chip in to help if you are really hungry.

Thuy and I did. And between the two of us, we made exactly three *buuz*, Mongolian steamed dumplings with meat stuffing, and that was for the purpose of getting a photograph.

After leaving Dalanzadgad, the emptiness of the Gobi becomes apparent. We passed a few other vehicles, mostly because it was high tourism season, but otherwise saw little of human presence.

Mongolia is a country of less than three million people and for each person there are five animals, most of which are roaming free across this vast and so incredibly beautiful country.

ꕤ

We appeared at our lodging for the night—a ger sitting by itself on the vast expanse of the steppe grassland, lived in by a nomadic family of four. Gers are the white portable houses that Mongolian nomads live in. There was nothing to be seen for miles, not even the top of another ger till horizons end. It was ethereal, to say the least. I had never seen or experienced anything like it and I can pretty much say the same for the others as well.

After dropping us off at the ger, our driver headed away into nowhere, to his village apparently.

'He will come back in the morning,' Bazo the guide assured us.

The first wave of being completely isolated hit us just then. What if something went wrong? What if there was a medical emergency? What if…what if…I suppose these doubts are natural. There was so much empty space around that it was a little scary.

I singled out Thuy.

'Is there so much space in the world?'

'Yeah, there is. Mongolia is also sparsely populated which means all this is yours for the taking if you want, I suppose.'

Our welcome snack was dried curd or aruul, which after a long, bumpy ride was just the sort of thing that made us feel welcome and washed down by salty milk tea, everything felt all right. We spent a considerable amount of time understanding the making of aruul and helping the good lady in milking her goats. Being a small part of this nomadic life was fun and everything was fine till the realisation that a shower was not to be had sunk in.

I gave up trying to milk a goat when I realised I had to go to bed smelling of goat.

The ger itself was surprisingly large, comfortable and self-contained and had a TV, a small refrigerator and an old manual washing machine.

'How do they run the washing machine if they have no source of water?' I asked Bazo the guide.

He mumbled an answer that was far from convincing. I left it at that.

For a guide, Bazo was ill-informed, but he made up for it by playing regularly on his guitar.

'I don't suppose they wait for travelling horsemen or travellers to bring them news of the world any more,' I said to Thuy. 'How cool to find TV in the midst of nowhere. This doesn't feel isolated any more.'

Thuy had other important questions to ask Bazo.

'Do the children go to school?'

'Yes. Yes. In the village. They stay in the school. Like a hostel.'

Talk about change. This was evidence that Gobi was no longer isolated. Satellite TV and cheap solar panels have ensured that they no more rely on wandering horsemen or travellers to bring them news of the world. Tourism is on the rise, Gobi being the most often visited place on this side of Mongolia and yet the nomads are extremely friendly and giving. Friendliness is ingrained culturally among the Mongolians and the harshness of their daily life hasn't changed that unique quality.

That night under billions of stars, I realised what it meant to be at peace.

Briefly, I imagined what it would have been like hundreds of years ago during the time of Genghis Khan. How had he managed to round up the tribes to create the world's most powerful and feared empire? I half expected the ghost of the warlord to descend upon us that night—such was the influence of the desert on my mind.

The next day I learnt about *ovoo*, the Mongolian spirits that guide the travellers and ensure their safe journey.

We stopped at a particularly large mound of stones topped by a fluttering blue scarf. There were bottles with money in them, head of a goat, half bottle of Chinggis vodka and another bottle of milk.

'The ovoo likes stones,' explained Bazo, adding his share to the pile as he walked around it. I followed out of curiosity. 'The spirits can grant you everything, from a safe journey to a healthy son.'

I picked up three and followed him around the ovoo, adding my share as I went along.

'In India, we offer sweets, milk, fruits, turmeric or sandalwood to anything that is considered even remotely holy. Throwing a stone would easily cause a religious uproar. Should I say anything as I do this?'

'Repeat after me: *Big Ovoo is yours, big benefit is mine.*'

And so I did. *Big Ovoo is yours, big benefit is mine.*

'Stones are sacred here,' Bazo continued. 'The bigger the pile, the happier the spirit. Else, if you are in a hurry, you simply honk at the ovoo. It will understand your hurry. But you must acknowledge it.'

'Is it a religious practice or more of a cultural ritual?'

'This is a Shaman and Buddhist symbol. Also ovoo is a kind of border line of village and province. Mongolians also hope this will bring rain.'

First, I prayed for rain. And secondly, that we would come upon no road surprises.

I swear I heard the sour American girl on the tour, with whom I had had very little conversation, snigger as she watched us walk around.

My personal belief is that as a good traveller, it helps to keep an open mind, to be surprised and even shocked by other cultures but sniggering isn't the right thing to do. Tolerance towards other cultures is the primary courtesy every traveller should have.

My prayers may have taken a long time to reach, because soon after the engine over-heated. I was the first to know because I was the one sitting beside the driver and happened to put my hand on the mound under which the engine bubbled viciously while the clouds continued to form threateningly overhead.

The ovoo had clearly got my prayers mixed up but that's how I experienced my first rain in the Gobi. And because of that I ended up with a cold for the remainder of the trip.

In the days that followed, I learnt a lot about the desert and their way of life, despite the fact that our guide was generally ill-informed and the driver spoke no English. Sometimes you learn a lot just by observing and not getting into conversation with fellow tourists whose idea of a journey is to talk incessantly of other places they have been to.

From one breathtaking landscape we drove to another, fuelled intermittently by buuz, aruul, noodles with chunks of meat and potatoes and *khuushuur* (a meat pastry) washed down by milk tea and frequent swigs of *airag* or fermented mare's milk. We went through canyons, pitched our tents by the Ongi River, befriended sheep dogs, made campfires, exchanged news with the nomadic herders at water points, chased storm clouds and drove in the rains.

At one of these water points, we encountered modern technology.

A young herder on a motorbike after channelling his herd to the drinking trough pulled out a phone and began talking into it. When done, he asked me if I would pose with him for a picture.

I agreed.

And without a second thought, he pulled out his iPhone, set it to self-mode and got to work.

A selfie-enthusiast in the Gobi may be a little hard to digest, but to assume that Mongolia had not caught up with the rest of the smartphone-flaunting bandwagon would be to underestimate the advancement of Mongolia.

Smartphones have come to Genghis Land.

Hallelujah.

Few sights in the world have moved me to tears. Khongoryn Els in the Gobi Gurvansaikhan National Park, southern Mongolia did.

It was like something I had never seen before. I live in Dubai, a city that thrives on the fringes of the Arabian Desert and no matter how lost you are in the mountains of sand in your backyard, there is help at hand. You cannot remain lost forever.

But it would be completely wrong or out of place to speak of the Arabian Desert and the Gobi in the same breath.

Picture this—you are standing on the grassland, looking up at a vast expanse of sand rising out of nothing. This sand mountain is flanked by mountains. So in reality, what you are essentially seeing are three different geographical demarcations supporting different life forms. Up in the mountains which experience snowfall in winter, lives the elusive snow leopard while down the sandy slopes in the desert live the Bactrian camel with its distinct two humps. If that alone is not enough to move you, a walk up the sand dunes to what is popularly called the Singing Sands will move you in ways you cannot imagine.

Watching the sun go down on the steppes from the highest sand dune in the middle of The Great Gobi is enough to make you silent.

I'd happily go back to this place again just to watch the sands shift and sing in that peculiar piercing way that is somewhat like the music of a horse-headed fiddle. But it could also be my imagination. Gobi was like that.

⁂

While the sand dunes enthral, the ice blocks in Yolyn Am, also known as Vulture's Valley, shock. Ice blocks are hardly the thing one hopes to see in the midst of a valley in the desert, but that is exactly what you find here. Huge chunks of ice, sort of like a glacier, filling the narrow gorges. The ice apparently lasts for about nine months a year. The hike to the ice gorge is a little challenging though, but nothing that cannot be done even if you are a city bumpkin. I firmly believe that the trick to enjoying the beauty of the Gobi is not to expect anything.

I could write a book on Mongolia, given a chance, but that is besides the point. Of all the nights we stayed in gers, eating noodles and drinking milk tea, I wondered just what it was that made this journey so special. Was it the landscape? The people? The hardship? I hadn't showered in five days until we reached a small town with a public hot shower, but after the second day it hadn't mattered. From one beautiful landscape to another we had bumped along, seeing raw nature and trying desperately to fit into this side of nature.

When we arrived at Terelj National Park on the last day, things had changed. Being back in civilisation was unwelcome, despite everything that we had experienced in the Gobi. Lack of amenities hadn't mattered any more.

As far as national parks went, Terelj was definitely the tops, in the sense, it was well kept, within easy travel distance from the capital city and it also gave you the impression of being in the countryside. True, there were gers to live in, but it didn't feel the same. It did not have that rawness and that purity that came with the real nomadic life. Out in the desert, the gers gave off the feeling of belonging, the smells mixed with the smell of the steppes and cattle and bubbling milk had defined the journey. Here in the national park, that was missing.

༄

For Mongolians, Genghis Khan is a hero. That may or may not be the reason why everything in Mongolia, including the beer, vodka, candy and the airport, is named after him. Not surprisingly, after the fall of communism in Mongolia, a forty-metre-tall statue of Genghis Khan on horseback was built on the banks of Tuul River, which also happens to be the biggest equestrian statue in the world, a fitting tribute to the great hero who led one of the biggest empires in the world. It is said that Genghis Khan had found a golden whip in this very place. The statue is tall and wrapped in 250 tons of gleaming stainless steel and can be seen above everything in the vicinity.

It stands on top of the Genghis Khan Statue Complex, a visitor centre that itself is ten metres tall, with thirty-six columns representing the thirty-six Khans from Genghis to Ligdan Khan. The statue is symbolically pointed east towards his birthplace.

Inside the two-storey base of the statue, visitors can see a replica of Genghis Khan's legendary golden whip, sample traditional cuisine of horse meat and potatoes, or play billiards. Visitors can ascend to the exhibition hall using an elevator at the back of the horse and then walk to the horse's head passing through its chest and the back of its neck from where they can have an excellent panoramic view over the complex area and the scenery beyond.

To the outside world the statue might appear to be an excess, because there are varied opinions on the greatness of the warlord, with some swinging towards the notion that the conqueror was destructive and brutal.

But here I will stick to the fact that he was a hero, well, at least I grew up believing it to be so. Genghis Khan is also a larger than life figure and a symbol of Mongolian culture.

The Mongolian psyche and persona, as well as its fledgling tourism industry, appear to be based almost entirely on Genghis Khan and his exploits, from the name of the airport to his face on the currency and the most popular brand of beer.

No matter what the general opinion about the statue is, I thought it was worth every *tugrik* (Mongolian currency) to take an internal lift all the way up to walk along the length of the horse's mane.

It was the closest I could have ever hoped to get to the heart of Genghis Khan.

THERE ARE NO ROADS IN MONGOLIA

Whoever said there were no roads in Mongolia was probably only looking for a stretch of paved earth and thereby not seeing the green flower-covered hills and valleys and steppe with more herds of horses and goats roaming free. Agreed that the roads end some distance away from the city of Ulan Baatar and it is not easy to fix a location on a GPS if you have one, but then, Genghis Khan didn't have one either and yet he created the world's biggest and most feared empire. That is saying a lot, right?

Mongolia is still pristine, with its green hues, herds of wild horses and the expanse of golden desert. For me, it was an experience like no other. I lost myself as I travelled across its central and southern lands that took in everything from deserts, rivers, monasteries, flatlands and fossilised earth and with that I learnt to embrace the beauty that comes from simplicity and indulge in the overwhelming sense of liberation that comes only from standing in an uninhabited place. At night, the desert transformed into a huge planetarium. It was sheer bliss to see so many million stars so close to earth, to see shooting stars and wish upon them till you saw so many that you just ran out of things to wish for.

Mongolia is memorable like that.

An occasional horseman checking the livestock or just galloping across the land for the sheer joy of it is a sight that will remain with me forever. The horsemen on the steppe rounding their herd feel so much in tune with the nature around them, so unmindful of everything else, just belonging to the moment of oneness of man and animal.

Mongolia will make a horseman out of you. Even if you're inexperienced, galloping after spending half a day on your horse will make you feel like you were born to do this. Never mind your back and ass telling you later that you'd actually be better off in an office chair.

In Mongolia it is said that in life you should ride your invisible horse of luck.

The invisible horse of luck signifies your personal power and harnessing it will keep you safe, somewhat like offering stones to the ovoo. I can back it up with our own personal experience when the engine was over-heated. Had it bubbled a little longer, there was a good chance it would have blown us all into space. It was true what they said about riding the invisible horse of luck. In Mongolia it is also about believing in the inner power.

My time in Mongolia has been phenomenal, and I am immensely lucky to have had this experience. I came here with an expectation of arriving at the end of the world, and was pleasantly surprised to find it all. Don't get me wrong—there is a lot about this place that is old and ancient but there is also a lot that is familiar and comforting. And yes, there is that lingering smell of goat everywhere, but only just. That is how you smell your dinner and the beautiful cashmere you have come to purchase.

Today, I can say this with pride—I haven't been everywhere in the world but I have been to the Gobi. And I firmly believe there is no place on earth like it. Perhaps the Gobi steppe bears a slight resemblance to the African savannah but the landscapes make for a unique environment, and one made even more so by the Bactrian camel, an animal found nowhere else in the world.

The relationship between man and animal is the same as between man and his machine. Our guide Bazo told us that the driver considered the van to be his second wife! Agreed, the van was not exactly modern but its suspension can beat any modern day 4WD and what was even better was that it was easier to fix when things went south.

Of all the places I've visited in Mongolia, the Gobi is by far my favourite. Not because its any type of vacation, but because its forbidding beauty challenges the imagination, and because the Gobi people are the hardiest, yet friendliest people in the world.

Mongolian countryside is practically unlimited. You can drive for hours and hours without seeing anyone or anything but grasslands and mountains, horses, sheep, cows and eagles. So when you see the top of the white ger in the distance your heart leaps with joy. The desert brings out the real you. You also realise that it is not the lack of roads that keep people away because here, people are outnumbered by livestock and yet, they know exactly where the next ger is and the shortest way to reach it. They are nomads, yes, but they are social and generous.

I can't understand why people run down a place that does not match a non-existent culinary standard. So never mind if you have heard that Mongolia is no place for vegetarians, and that you can make a list of all local dishes and each of its variations and still not cross fifty varieties in all. Be assured that food here is wonderful, despite the repetitions you might find every day. Vegetables are limited to a few, but really, you cannot blame the locals for the country's climatic conditions, right?

I found it particularly offensive when one of the members of the trip insisted on shaming the local cuisine, saying, 'Eating so much meat is turning me into a barbarian.' Well, that just goes to show how immature people can be in their thoughts. As a first time visitor, you might initially find the meat a little too much, but that meat and all its fat is necessary to see the Mongolians through their harsh climate. Mutton soup, mutton pasta and mutton risotto, old mutton, young mutton, smelly mutton, fatty mutton and even smellier mutton are all a part of the daily cuisine, changing according to season. Occasionally you will have some veggies as well.

ନ୦ଔ

I have not touched upon Ulan Baatar, keeping it for the last. As you can see, the great Mongolian outdoors have influenced me much. As a rule, I avoid the city as much as I can, but in Mongolia, I made an exception. I admit, here, I surprised myself. I really like this city. It is easy to get around, either by a bus, taxi or if you like, walking. I did a lot of walking here. That way I discovered that even here there was no escaping the kimchi!

I say this in jest, of course. But coming to terms with the fact that a variation of kimchi is a delicacy in Malaysia, Singapore and Japan was hard because after North Korea, I was not sure I wanted to let go of my deep-rooted dislike for this dish which seemed popular elsewhere too.

Like every other capital city, UB has a fair share of top-end restaurants, dining spots, a variety of cuisine, shopping centres and coffee shops. Okay, even if for a moment I had nursed any misgivings for being in UB, it dissipated as soon as I discovered the excellent coffee shops here. I am not a restaurant snob, but I could be called a coffee snob. But even I will get off my high horse and say some of the coffee I had here was by far superior to the

Starbucks or Costa I am used to. I even gave Korean food a shot—with the kimchi and all. I have my mind set about kimchi, but in UB, I fell in love with *bibimbaap*, Korean mixed rice with meat and assorted vegetables.

What surprised me most about this city was that culture shock was almost non-existent. I suppose their friendliness breaks down this barrier quite easily and because people come here with a determination, that quality lends itself to some great possibilities.

Catching a cab here is an endless pursuit of pleasure. It really is. I love catching a cab in UB—you just hold out your hand, someone rolls up, you hop in, they take you where you want to go. If you are lucky, they won't rip you off. In places where cabs are 'official', the element of the unknown has been removed.

I would have loved to stay on longer, to hire a car and just drive into the horizon. To hell with the roads, here I could have learned to drive like a Mongol. Ride a horse like them—who really cared where you went?

The countryside. My mind always wanders back to it. And the people. Okay, I am not the biggest fan of Mongolian food, but I have grown to appreciate meat. I don't eat a lot of meat back home but here I actually loved the bland, fatty meat I had with every meal. I really miss the place a lot. I suppose there is always the chance of returning, but the mix of people will be different. I hope when I do, Mongolia would have changed that much.

When I think of Mongolia these are what I think of and in no particular order:

The weather. It is really quite fantastic. In the summer time, it's mostly sunny and warm, but never humid. The skies are blue, the grass is green, and even though there is more dust than I would prefer, the scenery is amazing. The city is a great place to sit on a patio and drink a beer and the countryside makes for some great outdoor activities.

The fashion scene. It's bold, quirky, and totally Mongol. The women look amazing. Of course, with their fair skin and bright dresses sometimes a bit overboard, but the love affair with knee-high boots and bright colours will be missed.

The expat community. It's a small community here, with everyone knowing everyone. Because of that, I think it's easy to make friends, easy to find things to do, and easy to fit in. And, with some of the friendliest, most amazing people, it's something I'll really miss a lot.

Fresh dairy. I love the dairy in Mongolia. It tastes like grass.

North Korean food. Not that it is all that different from South Korean. There's just something about eating in a restaurant run by North Koreans that is maybe a little bizarre. Especially if you have just arrived from that very country and it has left a slightly disturbing influence on you.

Also, the food is AMAZING.

Mongolia is not your standard high-class go-to-the-beach and take-it-easy holiday destination. If you like adventurous travel, love nature and are not afraid of some cultural experiences, Mongolia is definitely the place to go.

And better still, there are no beach bums in Mongolia.

A FAKE MUZUNGU – ME

Until I had set foot on Ugandan soil early one morning and walked into a two-metre, wooden-faced, ebony-skinned Ugandan, I didn't believe I would ever appreciate the ostrich's need to bury its head in the proverbial mound of sand. I had run face first into the monolith's chest area reeking of stale sweat and if that was not embarrassing enough his plucking me away as he would a praying mantis, before I could murmur an apology, reduced me to dust.

But the first words I uttered were 'Yuuuuccccks'.

I was mainly referring to the smell of his chest.

The monolith looked down at me and asked an unpleasant question.

'You want black man?'

I swear if there was a grain of sand at hand, I would have buried myself in it. It could have been his voice or something else but that question knocked the wind out of me and with it, the sarcasm that I bank on. It took me a few seconds to revert to my thick-skinned, indifferent self and as a knee-jerk reaction I let a fake happy smile appear.

His was a face that didn't give free run to emotions. The poor airport parking lights didn't help his features much and unable to guess his intentions, I let my smile be. You couldn't peg me down as the unsmiling type, because, fake or not, I smiled a lot.

The Tower spoke again—

'Muzungu ladies like black man. Yes? Maybe you want man also? Muzungu like black man. I bring you one.'

'No. Me no like black man mister, no like. Sorry, you got the wrong muzungu.'

'You white bitch,' he hissed out suddenly and unexpectedly. The man-tower really needed to work on his manners. Such a cut and dry sort of attitude was not going to help his pimping career. In the general sense, I was not a *muzungu,* because the real specimen, I happened to know, had lighter skin with perhaps gold in the hair and blue in the eyes. No matter how desperate you were to stick a man in my face, no pun intended, there was nothing muzungu about me. I have a healthy shade of brown so uncommon to the muzungu, and I do not believe in picking up men at airports for a roll in the sack. I am a backpacker all right, but you could give me some credit for being able to pick the men I wanted to be slutty with!

I smirked. When sarcasm fails, this is what I do. Smirk. That's Plan B. A smug and condescending smirk has always succeeded in reducing anyone to smithereens and eased me out of tight or embarrassing spots wonderfully.

'Go, find someone else to bother. Go away.'

The monolith whimpered and growled and backed off while I turned my attention to a cab.

I cannot explain why I looked up at the sky when I should have been looking at the cab that was crawling towards me, but I did look up at the sky.

A big billboard at the corner of the parking lot that covered half the sky had lit up. On it was a picture of a very dark, bald and mean-looking chap with a very shiny forehead leering down at a scared little girl. There was a message too, placed somewhere near the scared little girl's head—

Is this man sleeping with your daughter? Then why are you sleeping with his? Get off the sexual network. Get tested for HIV and lead a healthy life!

There are probably subtler ways to drive home the point of safe sex, like politely worded brochures handed out at the airports, but putting up monster posters that put the fear of the virus in you showed how serious they were about issues that affected their country.

A bold, smart move, I thought to myself shuddering just a little when the seriousness of it hit home. There is definitely NOT going to be any sheet-soiling for me here. No way, sir!

The billboard flashed again. Never mind, you lose some.

I hailed the cab. There was a lot on my mind—of various levels of importance.

ഇരു

Red Chilies Hideaway, Kampala was a name that came highly recommended by backpackers trawling the internet for cheap stays. I had quite liked what I had seen in the pictures and directed the cabbie towards it. The cabbie apparently knew the place and promptly loosened up and indicated his desire to talk by coughing unnecessarily.

I obliged. I am a very accommodating traveller that way. And Kampala was forty-five kilometres away.

I opened the conversation.

'Crazy. That fellow back there? Crazy. And rude, damn him! Did you see what happened?'

'Yes, yes, I saw that. Not good, that man.'

'Ah, you did? Rude, wasn't he? I mean, what the hell? Is he here always? He was trying to fix me up with some random bloke.'

'Yes, always. Many, many others like him. It is very common here in Uganda. He asked you for a man? Many pimps near the airport. The government must do something—it brings Uganda a bad name. You must be careful.'

He said it with so much feeling that I believed him. The conversational ball was on the roll.

'Where do you come from?'

'Dubai.'

'Arab?' His voice gave away the disbelief. 'Dubai? Oil country?'

'No, Indian living in Dubai.'

I let it pass that Dubai, my adopted Sunshine City, had no oil worthy of mention. Abu Dhabi had all the oil. Dubai had the swanky shopping malls and Range Rovers and the tallest building in the world, but not enough oil to show off or to hold the Ugandan cabbie's attention.

'Too much Indian here in Uganda. Too much money, huh?' this followed a suggestive wink. I don't know why he made out money to be lustful, like something to be leered at, but I let it pass.

'Yeah, maybe. I wouldn't know.'

'No, too much Indian here doing business. Very nice people, make too much money, big houses.'

I had no interest in money-making Indians. They were everywhere and as far as I was concerned, if I wanted to feel like a stranger, the less I saw of my fellow countrymen the better chance I had of feeling like one. It is that feeling of being in a completely alien country that widens the scope of your exploration of the new country.

'Why do you go to Red Chilies? There are many, many good hotels in Kampala. Red Chilies too many Western people—very cheap there. But, no problem, it is good…'

I stopped him midway to tell him that I was going to Red Chilies for that very reason. How had he not picked up on that?

I looked like any other cheap-ass backpacker—the kind that the commonplace swindlers, pimps, cabbies and ambitious people usually left alone. Usually. Not always. I even had the kind of early morning smile exclusive to travellers, which said they believed that the world was a kind place, people were kind and eventually they would find a cheap B&B somewhere.

What had made the cabbie think I was Miss Moneybags?

'I have no money, my friend. Red Chilies is cheap, I want a cheap place. Hostel, preferably. No money. I have to stay here for three weeks.'

He smiled. I knew he did because that precise moment I turned towards him and saw his teeth flash in the darkness. It was a smile, all right.

'No money, ha…ha…ha…Arab country too much money.'

And he laughed. And because there were only so many times I could say 'no money', I let it be.

The rest of the journey passed in relative silence though every time we passed small towns with street lights, my eyes always fell on posters about HIV and I began to see a hidden agenda in the electricity board's decision to light up certain boards and not others. But it had pretty much driven home the point of the electricity-eating campaigns against sex.

Not a bad use for electricity, I say.

ஜ

There was no obvious link between its rather spicy name *Red Chilies* and the camp itself, and at eight dollars a night for a dorm, it was not cheap either. The beds sagged but you could be an over-the-top optimist and take a very positive view of that. The truth is that one didn't go to a dormitory in Kampala expecting to find a spanking new bed.

And what was that story about the sagging bed and condom wrappers lying about?

I found myself an empty top bed and settled down, wrapping up in the flight blanket I had had the foresight to pinch because the sheet that should have rightfully been mine was hanging loosely around a bed as a sort of curtain behind which someone may have scored a number.

Things were peaceful till about 8 am when the bed beneath me shook violently. I am not sure if I should have bothered to peek over the side but I did and was not surprised to see Tomas, the receptionist who had checked me in, leave with a very satisfied smile on his face.

Pre-dawn romps were very much the norm amongst the travelling community that lived in cheap dorms and I had experienced it in the past. This usually followed animated discussions of it over breakfast which often ended in exchanging partners. I would eventually hear about Tomas because someone would show off sooner or later, which meant if the verdict was favourable, Tomas was up for some action the following night as well. It worked like that, always.

I didn't think it was likely that I would ever be surprised at what travellers did, but I was always surprised, despite being exactly like any other traveller. It is a matter of getting used to.

The eagerness to explore the neighbourhood and need for breakfast took over and I strolled out of the wrought-iron gates of Red Chilies, manned by a stone-faced security guard. I was fresh off-the-flight and thus full of eager anticipation and happiness, so I smiled and unnecessarily asked him for directions to a restaurant despite his unhappy expression.

What I didn't expect was a guffaw and sudden hand-grabbing followed by a vigorous handshake and sudden burst of information.

'Welcome, welcome. I worked with Indian family before, in Jinja. Nice, Indian, welcome welcome.'

I wanted to ask him how that answered my questions about the restaurant, but held my tongue.

'You know Idi Amin? He make all Indians go. So I come to Kampala to work.'

Of course, I knew of Idi Amin. I nodded pleasantly despite not having had my coffee and no directions to a feeding spot.

'Oh, how sad,' I tried to put feelings into these seemingly meaningless endearments. That encouraged him to get into details and just as he was about to explain why the dictator-tyrant drove away the Patels, forcing them to abandon their big bungalow, I escaped with a 'tell me all about it later'.

Being an Indian eager to talk, I had reasons to fear that everyone in Uganda would somehow assume my interest in their sorrowful history. It was not a pleasant thought.

The guard called out after me—

'Indians are coming back again.'

That didn't sound very promising either and because I couldn't see his expression through the back of my head I found that statement particularly ominous.

My dad had told me stories about Idi Amin, going as far as adding a 'sighting' of him at some airport in the Middle East some years ago, which to my young ears had been the most interesting bit—but that is another story. He could easily have made that up, but from what scraps of conversation I had heard from people over the years that included passionate and often heated discussions about the economic war of 1972 that pretty much cooked the goose of thousands of naturalised Indian-Ugandans, I had unknowingly built an image of Idi Amin in my mind and eventual research and information I gathered on the internet supported that fact.

Idi Amin certainly had been quite a character and the more I thought of him, the more I wished I could have met him in a dark alley.

Finding a restaurant in this part of town required walking up and down uneven roads packed with *boda bodas*—motorbike taxis for the newbie—spewing petrol fumes in your face, the persistent blaring of horns, the clutter of run-down cars driven by devil-may-care drivers, chattering school children and the arrogant pedestrian weaving through the commotion on the roads. It was not as though walking through this nightmare guaranteed a restaurant where I could sit down to a meal, for on this side of town, restaurant meant an eatery by the road with a gas stove hissing out a welcome along with supporting the weight of a heavy iron griddle on which *chipathis* cooked in one corner and eggs in another.

The restaurant I found was the same as every other, limiting my choice to chipathi with beans, chipathi with eggs and Rolex—a chipathi wrapped around an omelette. There was no escaping the chipathi in Kampala, a legacy of the Indians who came to Uganda years ago with their chapathi. Idi Amin may have shooed away the Indians, but he couldn't kill their flatbread which eventually overthrew *posho* (a starchy meal made of maize flour or cornmeal, and millet flour and is a native east African dish) as the national dish.

On my order, the spatula-wielding cook-cum-waiter sweating over the stove tore up a chipathi into shreds, tossed it into a plastic bowl, threw in two slices of unripe tomatoes and slapped the resulting mix on my table, while the beans continued to cook and bubble on the side. It took four painful minutes for the beans to appear on my table. Four minutes on a hungry stomach can be excessively annoying, but I will admit that the beans had cooked well. I fell in love with the Ugandan beans.

Uganda may not be counted as Africa's culinary destination, or hold any appeal for a gastronome or set the average tourist's blood flowing at the mention of its food, but it knew its beans well.

In no way can I be considered a history buff. My interest in the historic past is limited to a photograph taken beside a tomb or a monument or say, old signboards and milestones because it helped remember names I could not remember. So I decided to surprise myself with a visit to the only existing proof of Ugandan history—the Kasubi Tombs.

Tomas, the smug receptionist didn't quite see what I wanted to do with his precious tombs; for that matter, nor could I, but between breakfast and nothing to do until the next morning before heading out on a safari, I had about twenty-four hours and I wasn't going to spend that time in the dorm watching raunchy backpackers at their mating games.

'Today is Friday,' Tomas said sadly. 'Why do you want to visit the tombs?'

'I am not sure, perhaps because today happens to be a free day for me?' I suggested. 'And what happens at the tombs on Fridays?'

He shrugged. 'Nothing much to see. You go to the mall. Or the pub. Kampala has many pubs. Very good.'

I didn't see how that helped at all. To begin with, I did not want to go to the mall or the pub and the underhand manner in which he tried to warn me off the tombs, fuelled a rebellious streak in me. I wanted to see the tombs, no matter what—and on a Friday.

'How do I get to the tombs anyway?'

That's how I met Sandy, the boda boda man, who hung about Red Chilies and came highly recommended by Smug Tomas.

Sandy knew the short cuts and twenty minutes later we fetched up at the burial site of the Kabakas, the kings of Buganda which is a sub-national kingdom enjoying autonomy from the State. Interestingly, all of Uganda's history is encompassed within this burial site and because I was not sure what to expect, when I walked through the Bujjubukula or the gatehouse made of wooden columns, reeds and thatch hut and ended up at the

Olugya, the main courtyard, I felt as though I had walked into a living museum.

It was a Friday morning and I bring this up for a reason.

I should have been on my guard when the smiling guide-cum-receptionist-cum-caretaker seated in the room full of colourful paintings made on bark cloth threw me a sarong and encouraged me to wear it right away. It was not as though my legs weren't pretty, they are quite appealing I have been told, but because female visitors were required to cover their pretty legs so as to avoid temptation. At this point, you may ask—'*Tempt whom*?'

I was only about to find out the answer to that. The guide continued.

'You cannot enter the Drum House.'

'Why?'

He slipped on the guide-mask.

'The Ndoga-Obukaba (Royal Drums) are played when a Kabaka is crowned or when a member of the royal family arrives or departs; or when a family member dies. The drummer doesn't get married either. He is a celibate, so you cannot enter it. It distracts the drummer.'

That answered my questions about female presence in the hut. A woman showing off her legs in the house of celibates sounds screwed up anyway you looked at it. But that didn't shut me up. I continued.

'Are there any drummers today?'

'No.'

'Huh?'

'This place is sacred,' he repeated a tad bit firmly. 'And today is Friday. You must not enter the hut.'

'Uh okay.'

I was beginning to dislike Friday altogether.

I wrapped myself up in a faded orange sarong and stepped into the courtyard letting my eyes sweep across the huts lining the compound walls. The guide appeared at my elbow and gestured expansively.

'There,' he pointed to the centre of the courtyard, 'there was the Muzibu Azaala Mpanga before the fire destroyed it. Bad, very bad. Everything burnt. Gone. It is on the UNESCO World Heritage List in 2001. You find it on the internet.'

Muzibu Azaala Mpanga had been the dome-like structure from the picture I had seen on the walls of the tiny reception area under which the four former Kabakas (Muteesa I [1835–1884], Basamula Mwanga II [1867–1903], Daudi Chwa II [1896–1939] and Fredrick Walugembe Muteesa II [1924–1969]) had been buried.

He continued. I detected a series of emotions in his voice, going from excitement when explaining the history of what was once there to misery when the subject of the fire that destroyed the tombs came up.

'The tomb was made with wood and reed and the thatch roof went all the way down to the ground. It was very interesting and sacred. The fire took it all away.'

Fortunately he abandoned the dramatics and showed me a series of scattered buildings and graveyards located behind the tombs.

Interestingly these buildings housed the descendants of the kings' former wives or widows—the keepers of royal secrets—but it might not be really fair to judge them by their living standards. I saw the 'royal' women tending to cassava and yam bush, calling out to each other in some strange language and pointing towards me, shouting out what I thought was a greeting.

I waved back cheerfully and thus got invited into the royal hut for tea made on wood fire in the common kitchen which was held together by ropes and vines.

Royalty here wasn't always about the crowns and jewels. It was about having a roof over your head, about the cows and pigs and cassava plants and being able to afford tea with milk.

'The Kabaka visits his wives often,' explained the guide as we entered the hut of the piglet-gathering woman who happened to be newest bride and the Kabaka's favourite. 'She is very lucky because the Kabaka makes a weekly visit to her. All other queens are jealous.'

He smiled as he said this.

'If she is queen, is that toothless little fella playing with that plastic toy a little prince?'

I do ask the most illogical questions at times.

We became friends after that. The tea had way too much milk and I dislike tea and milk altogether but nodded vigorously when the queen pressed the second cup on me. Guests were rare and it was an honour to welcome them into their huts. But it annoyed me a little when the queen tried to kiss my cheeks after I refused the third cup.

'She is very happy today. Today is Friday,' the guide explained. He didn't have to spell it out but he was being a good guide.

I finally ventured to ask the question that had been bothering me.

'Why is Friday so special?'

He broke into a smile, looked me up and down and smiled some more.

'The Kabaka visits every Friday—today,' and threw a quick glance at his watch and proclaimed, 'It's about time too. If the Kabaka sees you or any woman here and he likes her, he can take you as his bride. You will get a dowry.'

He sounded hopeful at the prospect of presenting me as a new addition to his Majesty's harem but it was enough reason for me to leave as quickly as I could. The Kabaka may have been an open-minded polygamist unmindful of his bride's nationality or religion, but my idea of a royal life did not include milking cows and tending to cassava plants.

We hurried through the remaining huts with interesting reed patterns but not fast enough to escape the entourage that suddenly appeared at the gates, although by sheer good fortune, I managed to squeeze through unnoticed.

ꙮ

I had learnt of Murchison Falls National Park on Google quite by chance. A series of clicks and a whole new world had opened up and MFNP didn't seem quite as removed from the trodden-path as one would imagine of a park in Uganda. In fact, Winston Churchill and celebrity writers like Ryszard Kapuscinski and Ernest Hemingway had wandered around the national park many years before I was born, which sort of made things seem better than they were, although if I were leading by Hemingway's example, I had a lot to be afraid of. Hemingway, according to history, had walked the Murchisons Falls corridor with disastrous results. But what was good for Hemingway and The Bulldog was good enough for me (I swear I hadn't heard of Ryszard Kapuscinski until that moment). With help from Red Chilies and encouragement from Smug Tomas, I signed up for their three-day budget trip into the Ugandan wild.

MAURICE AND A SILVER RING

The following morning I joined six other people in a slightly modified matatu that we hoped would safely see us through the Ugandan wild.

Matatus, as matatus will, are prone to the following—frequent breakdowns, leaky petrol tanks, flat tyres, occasional jamming of the gears and seat being dislocated on the application of dysfunctional brakes. The windows either do not open or do not close, but I took solace in the fact that I had a window that didn't close. It was hot. I positioned my body in a way that allowed my head to stay out just enough to get the wind on my face. I also learnt really fast that shut mouth was the only way to prevent eating dust and praying was an excellent way of ensuring safety of self, co-passengers, road users that included animals and people and the matatu itself.

It really works.

Occasionally though I did taste Africa, for no matter how much I tried to keep my mouth closed, I was forced to contribute to the conversations inside the matatu. An open mouth in Africa catches dust quicker than the clichéd 'foot'.

It's the reality of Africa you must learn to love.

There are some other realities that one must know in order to love Africa. Here, knowing the distance from one point to the other is not a consolation because you will never get there in the time you have been assured or have mentally calculated. Under these circumstances you grin and bear but the great thing is that you have no expectations and are pleasantly surprised when you do reach after all, in one piece, despite the bad roads, no-roads, endless fuel stops or flat tyres.

When we reached Masindi, we had become acquainted with everyone else. Three of the girls were medical students doing voluntary work as part of their medical training, the couple was from Amsterdam and there was me. We may have been from different parts of the world in a matatu heading straight into the Ugandan outdoors, but we had been thinking the same thing—

Will we make it?

In Masindi our worst fears were realised.

'There are no roads from here, only dirt tracks,' the driver said sadly. 'This is your last stop. You eat lunch here. You buy water and snacks here. No other place sells snacks. Last stop. Hurry, you have half an hour.'

Hallelujah.

So we were going to rattle our way to the world's end. If we wanted food or water or a glimpse of what passed for civilisation, this was it.

I am not easily worried. But when the driver sounded and looked worried, I worried. So did the others. We lunched in silence, filled up water supplies and got a good look of what life outside the game parks looked like in case we were stuck there for a long time.

The town of Masindi wasn't much to look at and besides the driver's ominous declarations, what worried me was that I would go off the world map before eating *matoke,* starchy green bananas cooked and mashed into a meal.

I conveyed this to the driver who despite his sad mood was the only source of information.

'You find matoke everywhere. But hard to find in Kampala. You must try it here,' he said and walked off in search of his friends.

Matoke was popular this side of Uganda because the more urbanised chipathi didn't have many takers here. The good people of Masindi who lived on the fringes of the National Park raised bananas in large fields and preferred the wholesome body of the raw banana to the more tiresome chipathi.

Smart people.

I found matoke in the little restaurant where we lunched, but I followed that with posho and greasy chicken cooked with tomatoes and in a matter of minutes, regretted it all.

Raw bananas did not go down well with the cornmeal and chicken and because there was no clean toilet, the driver directed me to the 'bush toilet' after first confirming the nature of my business.

'Short call or long call?' he asked. It was rather embarrassing but this was Africa. And people were direct like that.

But eventually we rolled along.

I suppose here began some of the happiest moments in Uganda.

This was real Africa. The dirty bustle of faraway villages, the lush subsistence farms and small villages springing out of dry earth, rough roads, friendly people with a smell of their own, a mind of their own and a sense of time of their own completed the picture that many have dreamed of but never realised.

As we passed under scrawny trees shivering with the weight of bounding primates I even began to smile, unworried that I was breathing as well as eating dust and getting my clothes coated in a reddish powder, which wouldn't wash off very easily.

Not a great time to get into a laundry-centric argument because we had other things to worry about—like a flat tyre and the fact that we were running close to danger and had to reach camp before dark.

Most travellers, I learnt from the driver and the co-passengers, came to Uganda for the gorilla safari, but others threw in some chimpanzees tracking, bird watching, trekking the Rwenzori Mountains, Equator Point, rafting on the River Nile and visiting the source of the Nile into their itinerary. When summed up like this, it didn't seem like a lot—but it was. That is the thing about Africa. It is as different and as varied as nothing else in this world.

Medical students chose Africa as part of their voluntary projects. It was an easy place to find people in need and no facilities to speak of to fulfil that. That was also the charm of Africa. It helped you fulfil your need for doing things for the human race.

But that didn't explain why I always came back to this continent. Someone told me that if I had visited Tanzania or Kenya or even Ethiopia, it was the same as seeing 'all of Africa', but I didn't think so. Whoever said that hadn't set foot on this alluring continent.

Each of the countries that made up Africa was different. Take the three east African nations—Tanzanians liked Ugandans a little more than Kenyans who saw themselves as the 'ruler' of the three because of higher tourist footfalls, volunteers and charity organisations and because they were more often in the news, whatever the reason. Ugandans and Tanzanians did not place much trust in the Kenyans, who drew the last straw when it came to honesty. There were undercurrents but masked well. However if you cared to have a long talk with a local from any of these nations, they would instantly get into animated conversations, batter the other to the ground, bring up their national policies and worse, their food.

Uganda often got ignored, their sole claim to fame being Idi Amin and his atrocities and after him, to the more enlightened traveller, as the source of the Nile, but even that often got washed away when the confusion about the real Nile came up.

People hardly believed that the Nile was two different rivers and that one of them originated in Uganda.

But I was beginning to think that Uganda was more of the Real Africa. It existed beyond the glossy pictures in magazines. I could smell, taste and hear the real thing.

The camp was better than I expected, except the toilets were far away from the tents, but the beer was cold and the food was good, expensive but good. And there was a resident warthog named Maurice who liked cold beer.

Who can resist a domesticated warthog with a weakness for the bottle?

Deep in the Murchison Falls National Park in Uganda's northwest region, a flutter of activity announced the departure of the *African Queen's* majestic journey upstream to the Murchison Falls. The *African Queen* was a big boat with two decks and a well-stocked bar but was by no means equipped to deal with a beer-hungry mob and failed miserably at pacifying a particularly agitated and rather thirsty young man who complained about the beer.

But beer is not the reason for writing this.

Every female passenger on the *African Queen*, including me, had been wearing light cotton shorts of varying shortness that morning and perhaps had the slightly misplaced notion of getting a tan on a cruise as an added bonus. What we did not know was that short cotton shorts were not going to save us our asses from frying on the metal chairs left on the deck too long under the Ugandan sun.

Following this, some of the females vanished to the lower deck but Sarah and I and some of the brave ones held ground.

'I am not going to complain about a simple burn, no way. Look around, the view is fantastic from up here,' was the word going around the top deck.

No burn, no gain.

Someone passed sunscreen around. I think it was Sarah, because she had a face that one associated with kindness and I applied myself to protecting whatever I could of myself from the sun.

We left the pier, giving ourselves up to Mother Nature to treat us as she deemed fit. Whether she wanted to run us aground or tip us into the churning waters or simply make our jaws drop at the sheer magnificence she displayed was really up to her. But seeing that it was hard to pinpoint her agenda, we dutifully donned the lifejackets and held on to the scalding railings, pretending joy at the blisters that instantly cropped up on our palms.

As we cruised along, little chunks of earth broke free from the Mother and floated down river, the Nile crocodiles sunned on the banks, waiting for unsuspecting animals to fetch up to the water before launching an attack, birds chirped in the branches somewhere above…ignorant baby hippos broke away from their pods and wandered away…

I say there are no cruises in the world that can equal a Nile cruise—open skies above, the great White Nile below and wildlife all around. Okay, I haven't been on that many cruises to make an educated announcement but I am quite sure there is nothing else to match the wildlife or the sun or the sheer isolation of this place. Amazonian cruises are probably great too, I mean, considering the danger you could run into—but well, going on the Nile cruise was the best ever decision I have made in my life. This was the Nile. THE NILE. Whichever way I looked at it, I was convinced I was right.

I could never have imagined this vastness. It was mesmerising to have the world's longest river flowing around us.

I turned to Sarah. 'Those lovely little islands in the river… those lovely marshes. Why, I could live here forever. Maybe I should join the crew.'

Sarah said nothing. The thought must have occurred to, roughly, everyone on board, possibly with the exception of Sarah who was getting married in three months' time.

In the swamps, something moved but we never got close enough to see what. The sounds that floated up to us were enough.

'Do you think the crocodile got that animal?' asked Sarah turning red and pale. 'Oh how horrible. I wish we could do something? It is horrible, horrible.'

I wished I could explain to her why the food chain had to continue as it was till world's end, but she was shaken, so I let it pass.

It was hard to imagine a German getting into a state like that.

And suddenly around a bend, the Nile threw another surprise. The Murchison Falls appeared through vapour clouds as the mighty river pushed itself through a seven-metre gorge before plunging forty-five metres below.

The *African Queen* edged closer.

'Do you want to return or hike up to the Falls?'

'Hike, of course. No way am I missing that sight. It's hot but I am game. Let's go.'

Sarah was fit as a fiddle; me, not so much, yet I kept pace with her and the other hikers who got off at this point to hike up to the Falls.

'Do not get into the water, not even if you see a rainbow and want to catch it…'

It was the last thing we heard the crew say before the Nile drowned their voices.

We were quite drunk—up to our eyeballs would be a good expression to use—and turned into a commonplace loutish group that believed in drinking between drinks. I swear I have very little idea how our girl-group swelled up to accommodate sweaty, unshaven men reeking of smoke and beer, but all of us pretty much tumbled out of the van on all fours and crawled into the camp with the sole intention of drinking some more, loosely discussing, among other things, some of the National Geographic shots we had witnessed and the subject of who was going to pay for the beer.

No agreement was reached but the smart guys who kept the beer cold also knew how to keep a tab and wheedle the shillings out of us, so we really need not have worried about being without money at the moment. No one was going to get out of Red Chilies camp without paying their tab. That much was certain.

We had collectively concluded that drinking any more was not going to worsen the situation, so we lounged about the bar while the more drunken ones sloped over wooden benches and sang into the growing night with the faithful Maurice looking on.

Maurice the warthog wanted beer.

It was clear from his expression that he hankered for lager, looking particularly crestfallen when a bottle passed by him. To show his anger, he rolled his beady eyes and sniffed the ground before coming to sit by our side.

'Hakuna Matata…ha ha ha,' said one of the group members tugging at the little tusks Maurice was showing off. 'Maurice wants beer? Yes. Good. Then Maurice will get beer. Come, Puumba, come to papa. Hakuna matata, come on here…'

Maurice was a candidate for our friendship, but at this point I suspect we would have befriended Nile crocodiles if they came by. We watched as two of the guys held Maurice down while the third pushed a bottle into his mouth and tipped the cold brew into it.

Following this, the Puumba slowly got up and walked away with a satisfied look on his ugly face. I swear I saw him grin.

'There goes a drunken hog. Look at him go...have you seen anything like that? A drunken hog...ha ha ha...'

Some distance away, Maurice let out a snort and settled down for a long nap.

'Say, if beer can do that to a hog, it will be easy to tame the wild, right?'

I have no idea who suggested that because Nick the caretaker came around to brief us about the camp safety at night.

'Do not keep any food in your tent. Do not scream if you see a hippo. Do not use your flash if you want to take pictures at night.'

I think, with the exception of Sarah, everyone laughed away the warning. Sarah was not sharing my tent, an English girl was and I didn't get her name, but sometime in the night, we faced a full grown, two ton (or more) hippopotamus. Because we had full bladders and because she was not strong enough to hold it in while the hippo ambled away, I became the only person in the world to know her shameful secret.

Have I mentioned the way the campsite was laid out? It is about 300 metres from the bank of the Nile if you follow the hippo's path to the water. The canvas tents are arranged to one side of the thatched reception-cum-bar and behind the tents are the sturdier huts or *bandas* which the non-budget travellers can afford. Along the right side of the campsite is a track that you can mistake for a regular footpath, but which in reality is the hippo path. But often, hippos change tracks and walk right through the camp and leave through the main gate which is their shortcut to wherever they are going. There is no saying what goes on in the hippo's head so when facing one, it is best to slip away noiselessly. Red Chilies have however continued to exist despite this hippo threat.

The said hippo had changed its track and wandered into the campsite, pretty close to our tent. Fortunately they are quite blind and the only reason they don't charge through the canvas tent to trample you to death is because they think the tent is a wall. They stand there unmoving and when their brains start functioning again, move on to wherever fancy takes them.

Thus when the said hippo was thinking its way, we had opened the tent flap.

This is the situation Nick had warned us about.

Do not scream. Do NOT scream.

The hippo may have a barrel-shaped body but can outrun a human even with a speed of 30kmph—a darned sight more than I could even if I had a turbo engine affixed to my legs. So I stood my ground and held the pee in.

But she could not.

When we were out of danger, I returned to bed thinking of the hippo and the warthog and the crocodiles that lived in the Nile. Then I remembered *Lion King* and the haul of animals riding the ostriches in the movie.

That thought made me smile.

That night I learnt an important lesson. I also understood what wildlife photographers and enthusiasts felt when they returned to civilisation. Even my brief encounters had left me hungry for more.

൭൫

As agreed Siraji turned up at Red Chilies the day after I returned from Murchison Falls National Park. I had been really looking forward to seeing him. He was the only familiar face in all of Uganda and it had been jolly good of him to travel up to Kampala from Moshi, Tanzania, where I had first met him two years ago.

Siraji Said had been my guide on my Mt Kilimanjaro trek in the year 2010 and we had stayed in touch. Siraji had had a soft corner for me but I was very much a commitment avoidant and I was not eager to renew any romance with Siraji.

Siraji, who had no idea how my heart had changed paths, hugged me with a force I had quite grown out of. He was definitely leaner but looked just as roguish as he did two years ago. The OUTLAW tattoo on his arms was just as tempting as it had been back then.

'I love you, Anjaly baby. I missed you.'

'I missed you too, yeah, I did, really. Good to see you again.'

I had become quite slick at making up harmless lies or so it seemed. But one gets good at such things.

'I brought you a ring.'

'A what?'

'I want to marry you.'

'Marry me? What? You must be out of your mind…no, sorry, that came out all wrong, I mean, marry? Hope to God you are kidding, Siraji.'

Let me explain. In the last two years, I'd learnt that Siraji had two little girls studying in Kampala which he kept a secret from me, had an 'on and off girlfriend', and a big desire to learn Japanese and settle in Japan at some point in time. My own ideas of a future differed largely from this, beginning with the problem of learning Japanese. I had no desire to establish a mobile phone empire as Siraji did and spoke of so often in his mails and on Facebook. So I mumbled something in his ear and hoped that in the few days we would be together he would change his mind.

'I brought you a ring.'

'Uh oh—but you know I am allergic to metal. See—' here I pulled at my earlobes and let him examine it, 'See, nothing. Allergy.'

Lie. Technically, wearing a ring wouldn't make me his bride but it would be looked upon as some form of commitment. A casual promise made two years ago in the throes of passion and gratitude is one thing but to enslave oneself to someone is different. I am a commitment avoidant, but not a cold-blooded heart-breaker.

'But I love you,' he said again, although with less passion. 'I love you very much.'

He hugged me again, and this time while I did not resist, I may have cringed a little. And just as he was about to kiss the top of my head, someone coughed beside us.

Smug Tomas.

He couldn't have arrived at a better time. Siraji was being dense and unreasonable and that I couldn't handle. SO when Smug Tomas suggested upgrading to a private room, I shook my head firmly.

NO.

If Siraji was surprised at my decision to continue staying in the dorm, he did not show it. I didn't care.

A DIP IN THE NILE

Siraji and I, his passion settled to a tolerable level, left for Jinja on a matatu the next morning. I sat away from him. Ever since my rejection, he had given vent to his feelings in various ways and unnecessarily started an argument at breakfast over matatu vs hitchhiking. He won, but not wanting to give in, I wedged myself between the matatu driver and a large woman, unmindful of the gear poking into my thighs. He found a place at the back. Occasionally I looked into the rearview at him but he seemed occupied with his own thoughts and the traffic, so I turned to the woman beside me.

The woman was Stella. And she was the public prosecutor of Jinja, the town we were heading to.

That fine morning I came to accept that there was no escaping the law and that there would always be someone from the said profession waiting for me at the unlikeliest places at some time or the other—even on a matatu. I have great respect for the law and the people who work the legal machinery and will root for anyone who steers the legal wheels in the right direction, but bumping into these specimens so often has made me suspicious of Providence. Or Karma. Or Fate. It is not as if I am constantly on the lookout for them, it is just that they happen to sniff me out of the thousands of people around.

I am the passive arm of that body too but defected years ago to become a writer, but Karma is a hormonal avatar of the faithful animal and at every given chance, shames me into following a path from which I had wandered off. It's a battle that I have not lost yet but I am of the belief that if I ever was in need of legal help all I had to do was wave down the first car and I would fetch up a lawyer manning the wheel.

In the present, Stella was telling me why she was on a matatu and not in her chauffeur-driven, state-owned car and I came to the conclusion that her name had nothing to do with her profession. Stella was a name one readily associated with kind, slender women with bows belonging in the pages of Jane Austen, but that could be just my opinion. This matatu-riding Stella wore a business skirt. She carried a bag. She was curious. She did not wear a bow. She was not slender. And she did not belong in any novel. The good people of Jinja looked up to her powers of judgement.

And she had an opinion. Yet, she was kind. I could hear it in her voice.

Here I am going to make a slight detour in the narration because a certain question has piqued my curiosity.

Why are people kind? Why are people kinder towards single females travellers?

As a female this phenomenon intrigues me. I understand the bias towards females, but again, why the bias at all? I strongly maintain that solo male travellers are just as nice as female travellers because, travellers universally have a common mental makeup. In fact, at the risk of irking the female of the travelling species, solo female travellers are rather smug and uptight when compared to the males, so what is it about being a female that makes people ooze kindness? Or is it just me?

If it is just me, why is it just me? Actually, it can't be just me, for I have met solo female travellers with interesting 'kindness stories' to narrate.

So had the male travellers, for that matter. I have woken up years later feeling loved and blessed just at the thought that people had been kind to me on various occasions and when I least expected it.

So, why?

Was carrying a 'single' tag the clincher? Did the locals feel the need to mother a lone woman? Did the men think they could score easily by displaying kindness or sympathy? Why did people think twice about extending a friendly hand to a male but were willing to grab the female whole and take her under their wing?

Truth is that be it in Turkey or Timbuktu, I have found it rather easy to accept kindness from menfolk as opposed to women because for some reason I believe men are more fun and in the generosity department, there is no end to what they can do or will do. They like to show off a little, too, and which woman in the world is immune to the powerful, dominating male?

Well, not me.

It is a curious phenomenon for which I am yet to find an answer. Meanwhile, I was okay with Stella's offer of her car for a tour of Jinja.

Siraji and I went in search of the Nile in a car that had a driver, a rare luxury for a backpacker in Uganda.

There are two ways to get to the source of the Nile which is at the centre of Lake Victoria. One is to pay a shocking amount to enter the premises and then some more to get on a boat with security crew, life jackets and other passengers. The second is to walk down the old railway line reached by travelling over rutted roads past the Nile Beer brewery, bribe the security guard and hire a canoe. That is, if someone agrees to row you over to the island.

We found this route via Stella's driver, a local with a good sense who coaxed an unwilling fisherman to row us to the source of the world's longest river. As to the actual conversation I cannot say, but I am sure there was some offering of immunity 'just in case' because I was the guest of the public prosecutor. The canoe was the sort one left in the backyard and grew winter plants in or the kind of thing adventurous ones pushed to the water's edge and pretended to fish from. We clearly had placed our faith in the paddle-powered transport while underestimating the force of the Nile's water.

I went in first. Siraji sat himself at the back and picked up a paddle. From the expression on his face it was not hard to tell why. The fisherman dug his oar and pushed.

For the longest time it seemed as though we were going downstream with the current but after combined curses and furious paddling by the men we turned around and directed the canoe to our destination. The canoe had a leak and the combined weight of us sank it lower so much so that much of the Nile took refuge in the old canoe.

I looked heavenward and prayed.

It was a short, dangerous and not-recommended way of getting to the Nile's source. There are other less dangerous ways that cost more, is less fun, safe and doesn't make a believer of you.

I have a thing for water. It makes me lose my mind, so much so that I discard caution and proceed straight towards it. But here, I got as far as the edge of the island separated from the raging waters by slivers of hardy weeds only to realise that no matter how much I wanted to, swimming was impossible and the only way I could merge with the Nile was to lie down on the weeds and let the river flow over me.

The stones were slippery, the grass was high and the water fierce and rolling naked on the weeds wasn't the best pose to be photographed. What eventually forced me to abandon my naked frolicking was the stream of curious insects that crawled out of the weeds and marched over my body. I still have a few bite marks but today I look at it with pride.

But the feeling when the Nile washed over me was almost spiritual. Almost I say, because I didn't have a lot of time to lie there and contemplate—but I assumed that if I did have the time to contemplate I would have fully agreed to the concept of spirituality. I feel spiritual about the places I go to. I mean, while I am not actively looking for that feeling, it does descend on me occasionally and I will admit that for a moment, naked or not, I felt one with the moment.

I remember having a similar moment when standing on Uhuru Peak in Tanzania on a cold and windy day in the rainy month of March in 2010, but it didn't come close to the feeling I experienced in the waters of the Nile. On Mt Kilimanjaro I was incoherent, so it was the same thing as being a drunk prophet, but here I was in my senses, though not in my clothes. There was something in that moment that made me vulnerable and powerful at the same time—powerful because my being there was an example of nature's willingness to let me enjoy these little moments that would take up a lot of space in my memory and on paper and vulnerable because nature was big and I, a small part that made up the world.

It felt as though something strong had descended upon me, it was as though I was at the start of a very long journey, that some part of me would eventually find its way, miles away into the Mediterranean Sea.

The very fact that I was seeing and experiencing something new, added to the excitement. And when that excitement is present, even the goodness in nature is magnified a million times and that alone makes me want to seek more of it. I felt in control and that gave me a sense of being powerful. It made me feel beautiful from within. No pretense, no shame, no worries about the flab on my belly. I was stripped of all bondage and chains; I was free. That freedom translated into a more magnanimous outlook of the world. When the heart is free and so are the boobs, everything seems different, more beautiful because freedom also allows you to absorb a lot more of the world outside.

And then reality struck.

This was also the place where former dictator Idi Amin dumped the bodies of those he had killed. Well, okay, not at this exact point, but in some part of this Holy River and such a thought was enough to kill the moment and make me want to run far and fast.

Damn Idi Amin.

And to ruin whatever was left of the moment the canoe-man called out.

'Watch out for the tsetse flies and crocodiles.'

There must have been a reason he didn't tell me this earlier when I had been lying on the weeds which said a lot about his moral integrity. There were hidden dangers everywhere.

We returned the way we came. Only it was easier to go downriver. But when jumping off the canoe, I did get my feet wet and thus my shoes. And I wasn't happy at all.

Later that evening, which was not very different from the next evening with the exception of rafting on the Nile's scary rapids, Siraji and I feasted on Jinja's famous Rolex which was different from its Kampala counterpart. This one in Jinja had shredded cabbage and slices of unripe tomatoes in addition to the omelette and cost a meagre 700-1000 UGX. I think I liked that over the roast chicken, goat and beef that I couldn't tell apart. Seen in the dim street lights of Jinja, goats, cows or pigs hanging by their legs over a coal fire look similar but what really put me off was the smell of burning animal flesh.

That night at Jinja Backpackers Hostel, much to Siraji's annoyance, I played with Nash's hair that looked a lot like Michael Jackson's before he turned into a white woman.

BOLLYWOOD IN KAMPALA

Bamboo Nest is within walking distance from Red Chilies and if you followed a straight path downhill from the camp, turned right and walked uphill for quarter of an hour you could get there in under half hour, except when the weather was intolerable.

Like it was.

The heat was intense. The sun was merciless. It was dusty. And while I am used to all of this in Dubai, what makes it tolerable in my adopted city is that I don't actually walk on dusty streets. In Kampala it is a whole different story. In the end I hailed a boda boda which deposited me in front of Bamboo Nest on the assumption that it was where I was headed to.

'Muzungu like Bamboo Nest,' he added unnecessarily while trying to cheat me over the price of the ride.

'I am not a muzungu,' I replied, counting out the 1000 UGX very slowly and deliberately. 'I am Indian and I am not paying you 5000. Thanks for the ride.'

Bamboo Nest in Bugolobi is the place to chill for cheap after wandering around Kampala on a hot day. Additionally, it is the hub of local gossip in which you can participate even if you didn't know what you were talking about. Gossip here was free. All you paid for was chilled beer, pork and African music, the three most popular choices for any down-and-out soul at the end of a bad day. If you want to spice up the evening, there are other choices as well, because Bamboo Nest keeps a full bar and while I cannot vouch for everything, I found their vodka particularly effective in blotting out the pain of bidding Siraji goodbye that morning.

I go back to the morning of the day. It had been particularly stressful because Siraji had left on a sour note and I could only assume the reason, but I was sad to see him go nevertheless.

'I wish you a happy married life,' Siraji had said quite unnecessarily and walked through the iron gates without looking back. He had sunk into a state of lovelessness and sour mood but I had my own interpretation of the word love. It was crazy and weird the way people in this part of the world interpreted things.

Then Karen, my dorm mate, and I had made a morning of it by visiting the vastly confusing secondhand market named Owena that had more brands on sale than Dubai Mall, bargained the shilling out of everything that we did not want to buy before finally paying five dollars for a pair of Adidas shoes. Following that, we stumbled out of the maze of clothes and shoes and found a boda boda that drove us to a coffee shop ambitiously named *1000 Cups of Coffee*.

We hadn't walked into the café; it was more like rolling straight into it from where we fell when the boda boda lost its balance and tipped us over. Karen bravely sustained a cut but in the light of what was to come, we ignored the minor distraction and ordered coffee.

'I hate to say this, but no matter which way I look at it, local coffee is undrinkable—too milky and way too much cream that sticks to the lips,' Karen stated. 'I hate cream that sticks to my lips.'

'I agree. I hate milk in my coffee—imagine all that cream. Yikes! It's one thing to have milk but that much? And with all that cream? Could that be real cream, you think?'

'God, I just want coffee that smells and tastes like coffee. It's the only thing I want right now.'

'I hope these guys know their job,' I said hopefully. I had never known anyone else to be that fussy about coffee, besides me of course. I am no expert on coffee but I like a cup that smells and tastes good. I am okay without the Tim Hortons, Costa, Starbucks, Gloria Jeans or Caribou, but I like coffee capable of lifting me out of any mood the moment I smell it.

Yes, I always smell my coffee first. And I am also slightly fussy about temperature. I like my coffee hot enough to generate a little steam in the cup.

Karen was not that fussy and we bonded nicely over coffee which did taste like coffee and by late noon and half a dozen cups of coffee later, Karen and I had become inseparable and continuing with our newly forged friendship, we decided to split for a while and meet again at the end of the day and drink the night through a few barrels at the nearest pub.

Hence this story about Bamboo Nest.

Karen had not showed up and I was quite drunk and given up hope. Last minute changes were common and I was tired and desperate to eat anything that did not look like greasy pig parts because as I recall I had had a plateful of that, followed by a bout of vomiting, but that could have been the vodka someone paid for when chatting over the bar-counter. I will never know.

But because of this, I met Bobby.

When I stumbled out of Bamboo Nest and straight into *Aashiyana* that announced its business on a flashing board that said 'Indian Restaurant', an Indian man sauntered over to my table, turned on the fan and directed it full force at me before switching the TV channel to Hindi.

'Give me food. Food. Anything will do,' I managed before dropping heavily into the chair.

I think at this point I didn't even want to get into a conversation with anyone, even a waiter, but I did take the suggestion of a vegetarian plate meal, popularly known as *thali*, seriously and nodded agreement.

All I wanted was something to sooth the fire in my belly and something to soak up the alcohol and hold down the retch. I swore off Ugandan vodka until the meal arrived and I filled up on the assortment of vegetables served in small, round, steel cups.

As long as Uganda had restaurants that served Indian-style vegetarian meals, there was hope for the drunk.

The man who had suggested thali sat down opposite me and launched into a conversation.

'I am Bobby. This is my hotel.'

It was funny how Indians anywhere in the world said hotel when they meant restaurant.

'Oh, wow.'

I wanted to say something completely different, but offered my name. I looked sufficiently Indian as to quell any question that he may have had about my origins.

'Are you here on work or tourism? Do you like the food?'

I offered a brave but half-lie.

'I am a writer doing some research in this part of town.'

It wasn't exactly a lie. I am a writer, but not that kind of writer that gets drunk on field trips if ever there was such a thing. Bobby was easily excited.

'Reporter? Wow! That is good.'

'No. Like a writer. Writing a book. On Kampala.'

Now, that was a lie. Of course, I would eventually write about my experiences in Uganda, but a book on Kampala was not what I was aiming at. For that, there were the good old *Lonely Planets* and *Rough Guides* and numerous other books that passed off for a guide book, but that is a whole different story. Also, if I were indeed writing a book, I would have been far more sober than I was.

'Even better. I have never met a writer,' he declared at the end of a short mulling and pondering as his brain assimilated the info. 'Where are you staying?'

I told him.

'I will drive you there. It is not very safe to walk back alone, or take a boda boda.'

I was touched. First Stella and now Bobby. Kampala was overflowing with kind people. It was always heartwarming to see this side of human nature. A good world it was indeed. Perhaps my being a little tipsy may have added to the excessive gushing, but it was a kind world. Uganda had not lost its heart in spite of having gone through a phase that would have hardened an average soul.

Bobby was a talker. He jumped from one topic to the next with alarming speed but ended with Idi Amin, forcing me to pick up that thread in between mouthfuls of rice soaked in lentil and mixed vegetables.

'Did you not leave when Idi Amin ordered Indians out of here?'

Such a question, I knew would ensure a steady flow of conversation and I could carry on chewing the grub as Bobby filled the silence without noticing that I had drifted. Plus, there is something about the Curious Indian Syndrome or CIS that automatically makes you ask an unpleasant question, but Idi Amin somehow seemed like the kind of historic name that one liked to drag into a conversation that needed to go on for a while.

Bobby lapsed into momentary silence, took a deep breath and launched into an animated, one-sided conversation. At this point I might add that much of the affected behaviour was put up with the sole intent of impressing me, the writer, because he dramatised every sentence, made elaborate gestures, pulled a face, burst into laughter, stabbed the table, ordered more food and pulled at his hair regularly as if to drive home the point.

Every writer, at one time or the other, must have experienced such animation. People everywhere are keen to tell you about their lives if they know you are a writer and clam up if you are a reporter which is strange. Of the ninety-nine times out of a hundred, all a writer wants to do is fill the silence but finds it hard to get the subject to stop pouring out information. On the contrary ninety-nine times out of a hundred, a reporter is really interested in knowing more but finds it hard to scrape together any info.

'I did not leave,' he ended with pride and threw up his hands expansively. 'My family left, but I did not leave.' He then proceeded to use a particularly strong Hindi word that signified his dislike of the regime that forced his family to leave.

I left with Bobby half an hour later with promises of returning for his Friday Special meal.

But I didn't make it to Bobby's Friday Special, for that particular Friday morning I went to the Equator Point to see why people made a big deal out of Half-Earth points.

Come to think of it, it *was* a big deal. Imagine standing with your feet planted on both hemispheres with the centre line passing under you. Clearly, the hundreds of people sleeping across the line, standing with their legs apart, making faces, thumbs up or standing with their legs raised proved just that—it was a big deal.

Sandy watched as I patiently waited for my turn to pose. It was here that I met David, a UNPOL (United Nations Police) officer stationed in Sudan, visiting Uganda over the weekend.

His opening statement shook me up a little.

'Pardon my saying, but you do have nice legs.'

'Huh? What? Legs, oh yeah? I have been told that...Oh, thanks for the compliment.'

I suppose David was a natural at this and insisted on having a photo with me and half held me up as though I had my legs wrapped around him.

Only later I realised how creepy it seemed, but what the hell. It was only a picture.

ꙮ

What happened the next day would go down in my book of memoirs for many reasons. It was the hottest day yet in Uganda, a day in which the wise stay indoors and drink water. But as it were, I had just refused Stella's offer of driving me around, subjected myself to a constant argument with boda boda drivers and eventually collapsed on the sidewalk due to the heat. But despite all this, I had not seen the stupidity of remaining outdoors and decided to watch a Bollywood movie *Ek Main Aur Ek Tu* that I'd known to have been a disaster.

It was the day I seriously wondered what made great travel stories. I cannot be called upon to pass a verdict on the film because I nodded off just as soon as the film began. But when downing a cup of coffee from the vending machine, I did ask myself many questions. Is it a common practice among travellers to watch movies they could easily have watched and for free in their home towns? I had heard of travellers going to local stage shows and theatres and even libraries, but cinema?

Really? Yeah. Really.

To make up for the time lost at the cinema, I hired Sandy again and biked away to Entebbe and thereon to Ngamba Island to watch chimpanzees feed. It was, I think, the best USD 70 I had spent in Uganda for the four-hour lesson on chimps that was better than any info I had gathered through watching Youtube.

ꙮ

Bobby had planned my last night in Kampala which involved making the rounds of the city's pubs and, continuing in the role of a benevolent friend, agreed to pay the cover charges for every one of them. Funny how he'd never considered giving me a free meal, which, I think would have been a great ice-breaker if he was eventually expecting me to go pub crawling with him.

As a self-imposed rule, I dislike being in a state of inebriation the night before travelling because that makes me cranky but there was a certain appeal in the watering holes of Uganda that made me give in to Bobby's offer because, among other things, I did want to see that side of Kampala I had missed out on because of Karen. I had heard good things about Bubbles O'Leary and regular pub-goers staying at Red Chilies talked of it with reverence such as only a connoisseur can manage to infuse in a noun.

Bubbles O'Leary deserved every bit of the respect it commanded. A regular haunt for the expats of Kampala, this one was definitely the tops, although the speakers were too close to the bar which left the dancers rather deaf at the end of it all.

I don't remember why we left this splendid place for an African pub that had nothing whatsoever to do with the name it carried. Casablanca. This is a place you would go to for African hiphop, cheap drinks, local music, and if you are a female, local men. Because all I saw were western women and local men drunk to their gills and in various stages of undress and before long, Bobby made his move.

Strange how a seemingly innocent act of snaking one's arms around the other and leaning over the shoulder to whisper into the ear can transform a perfectly platonic friendship into an invitation for sex.

And suddenly I wasn't so drunk any more. And I didn't think twice before leaving Bobby with his hurt pride and a rejected manhood.

Just as I was finishing checking out of Red Chilies the next morning, Stella arrived with her driver, her son Daniel and daughter Emily, who weighed as much as I did. She was one of those kids that took a shine to anything foreign and insisted on sitting on my lap and inspecting my hair and earlobes. She was a healthy baby and I winced every time she good-naturedly slapped my face with her chubby hands.

'I think she likes you a lot,' Stella offered every now and then when she heard Emily's hands come down on me. 'She is not very friendly with people generally. She likes you.'

'Oh she does, does she? Well, what do you know! Kids are really funny, I say.'

Emily may have sensed the sarcasm because she slapped me again. When we finally arrived at the airport, I was glad to put a distance between us. She ruined the moment again by slapping me as I was hugging the angel Daniel.

Stella hugged me goodbye with promises of staying in touch forever.

I missed Stella from the moment her car disappeared. She had added that extra something which was instrumental in making my trip go from being nice to unforgettable just by being the wonderful woman she was, Emily included. If Uganda had such kind-hearted souls manning the wheels of their legal machinery, eventually everything would be sorted out. There was hope.

To this day, we are in touch.

What follows may or may not have been the story of your travel life, but if it is the former, you have my sympathies. If not, as one traveller to another, I wish that no misery ever touches your travel life.

I arrived at the airport gate to the news every traveller dreads.

Gulf Air had suddenly ceased their operations on the route.

Flight cancellations are common but what I presume is not common is arriving at the airport to be told that your transport won't be arriving. That moment I had many horrid thoughts running through my head and everything began with a 'what if' and didn't go beyond scaring me into meekness. When the airlines do the disappearing act on you, you feel as though you should hang up your sneakers and never leave home again. It's the ultimate cheer-killer.

'We mailed you the cancellation,' said the chap at Gulf Air office without sympathy. 'We also offered to rebook you on a different flight.'

'Huh! You did!' said I. 'You really don't expect passengers to be checking emails on their holiday, right?'

'We called you too—on the number you provided.'

'And what happened then?' I countered, trying to be sarcastic but that horrible feeling in my stomach took the edge off the sarcasm. I hoped in some twisted way that sarcasm or something close to that would somehow turn the situation in my favour.

'Oh, nothing, really. Because it was switched off.'

It was true. From the time I boarded the flight from Dubai over two weeks ago, my mobile phone had remained off. There were two reasons for this, but none helped the situation.

My flight had been cancelled. Just like that.

Suddenly the horror of being stranded in a country seemed almost funny. I mean, what if Stella came to fetch me? I would be reunited with the bonny Emily, wouldn't I?

That thought hastened me into action.

'I must get back today—no matter how. What do I do now?'

By admitting that, I had managed to transfer all my fears to the guy and conveyed that he and only he could get me out of this situation. He fell for it.

'I could put you on an Emirates flight to Dubai but that leaves in an hour and flies via Addis Ababa. But you will get to Dubai today. Is it all right?'

I could have kissed his feet.

'Yes.' But that answer came out very stiff and ungrateful-like. Not the best approach but he didn't really care.

He handed me a letter and I dashed through the immigration waving the paper ticket urgently at anyone who cared to let me pass arriving at the boarding gate only to be told that we had run into a delay because 'there was no pilot to fly the plane'.

'How did the plane get here?' I asked no one in particular but within earshot of a uniformed man. 'Someone flew it in, right? I mean, can he not fly it out or something?'

I had a lot to learn about the functioning of airlines—including why pilots were required to stick to the specified flying hours but my lack of knowledge did not stop me from mouthing my thoughts. I had a lot to learn like that.

The guy was in a funny mood because he condescended to answer.

'Oh yes, someone flew it here but that someone has exceeded his flying hours and airline rules do not allow him to fly again. But cheer up, everything will be all right.'

Of course, I cheered up at this suggestion. It is always very reassuring when someone in a uniform tells you not to worry. Correct?

At some point after we had crossed the one-hour waiting period, people started walking about angrily, cursing the world in general and the airlines in particular, going from snorting to huffing and offering expert advice on how it should be run.

'I will miss my connecting flight from Dubai,' one was saying. 'I have a good mind to speak to someone RIGHT NOW.'

'It is strange this happened with Emirates. It is one of the most reliable airlines in the world.'

'No pilot? How ridiculous is that? I hate missing flights, this waiting is worse.'

This is what I love about travelling—it gives you a glimpse into the minds of people.

I was uncomplaining because I would finally get to eat 'real' food on the flight. It was about time I cleansed my system of posho and matoke and bad coffee. I could wait.

Another hour dragged, the end of which brought forth the same uniformed man and I raised my eyebrows as he passed by me signalling an interest in knowing the latest about the Plane Without A Pilot.

'We will board in a few minutes,' he said solemnly and walked on.

ഇ

The Uganda experience has been great. I have a feeling I will come back again. True that Uganda doesn't concern itself with the tourist. The uninspiring cityscape needs a major facelift, but again, does it really matter? I think the trick here is to visit without expecting anything.

But being here was absolutely exciting. I can't say with conviction that a casual tourist would find it very attractive, because there aren't many touristy things to do and walking about in the city is not likely to get you far or keep you safe, but it does offer activities that beats the sluggishness out of the most inactive soul.

Uganda is a country of surprises. I will give it that. Who could have imagined the superb yet scary rafting? Or the national parks? Or the chimps? I have never seen chimps for real until I came here and where in the world could you expect to have a run-in with a hippo?

I suppose when you put on your old clothes and hit the road, you are setting yourself free and are ready for surprises. And when you are ready for surprises, your mind sort of stops expecting and eagerly waits for what is to come. Sort of like taking the bull by its horns and seeing if it will go right through you or stop the beat midway.

It is a huge relief to free yourself from the monotony of expectations of daily life. How do you say that you will love long and dusty truck rides unless you have actually been on one? I am glad I will not have those regrets.

MUSAFIR MEETS SMALL FISH

A euro country is, any way you calculate, more expensive than a dollar/rupiah/shilling/kina country and the conversions are particularly alarming when your income is in UAE dirhams, forcing you to cough up AED 5 for every euro if the exchange rates are in your favour. Mine was one such case.

Hitherto when travelling into a dollar country, accommodation had been affordable—that along with my knack of sniffing out three dollars bed-and-breakfast accommodations ensured that my wallet had never required much stretching. But in Turkey, my wallet was likely to wear out with just looking at a living quarter, let alone live in it. Here, the cheapest, off-season rates hovered between eleven and fifteen euros, which was more than I had ever paid or was willing to.

My reason to visit Turkey was to see the 1800-year-old Sumela Monastery in an extreme corner of a vast country. Yes, reasons vary. Sumela Monastery was that variation.

I was also keen to try couchsurfing of which I had only recently heard about, but which promised to solve my accommodation issues. Couchsurfing, my research revealed, was the traveller's ultimate adventure, testing the ability to enjoy hospitality of strangers, to accept everything new and challenging, honed social and networking skills and educated you in the effective use of charm when things went south.

When I registered myself, I was initiated into a whole new world the good Casey Fenton had started way back in 1999 after fifty kind-hearted students had volunteered to put him up on his trip to Iceland.

God bless you Casey Fenton and I hope the fun and cheap ways you created for shoe-string travellers make it possible to dream of more fun and cheap travels around the world. Thank you!

Couchsurfing thrives in more than a hundred thousand cities, has millions of registered users, double that number of people who have already used the services, so there was only a one in a zillion chance that I could end up with a murderer, rapist or a thief. I was definitely no novice to shy away from such a challenge.

It had made inroads into Trabzon too.

The few people I discussed this with did not see why I wanted free stays with strangers and promptly delved into moral issues.

'Does that mean you get to have sex with them all?'

'Why would I travel to the end of the world just so I could have sex with a stranger, because hey let's face it, it just doesn't add up right?' Or 'Maybe I would couch with a girl? Where does sex come in here?'

Odd how the idea of free sex was always interesting to someone who'd never tried it and odder still was why the non-risk takers always used it as a weapon to destroy a poor soul merely looking for a free place to crash in and, in all honesty, looking to save a few dollars?

Why did the mention of a free stay send people into animated moralistic speeches, with sex topping the suggestion or outcome, followed by rape, murder, gay/lesbian angles, and drunken addicts? It was not as though suddenly everyone in the world who had spent considerable time uploading their profiles and pictures and writing about themselves had done so with some nefarious purpose.

I wasn't some sort of a tramp and no matter how much people arched their eyebrows and gave me pointed looks, I would still do it. This was such a dollar-saving deal and God knows how I needed to hold on to my purse-strings. There was nothing twisted about couchsurfing.

And that is how I met İbrahim Çavuşoğlu, a young Turkish doctoral student at Karadinez Technical University, Trabzon, Turkey. We became Facebook friends and in the weeks before I left, we had become really good friends. All that was left was to see each other and figure out if we were going to remain friends.

I further trawled the internet for free stays in places I was likely to visit in Turkey and drew up men and women eager to provide a bed. I am not sure whether it was my ethnicity, gender, travel portfolio or my job profile that attracted them, but I like to think that all four factors contributed. As a couchsurfing newbie I had no qualms about putting myself in the homes of strangers or living off their generosity, but then I had stopped being diffident years ago, so there was no reason to get all knotted up and bashful.

And with that in mind, I left for Turkey. It was the month of December.

When waiting for my Pegasus flight to Trabzon at Sabiha Gokchen International Airport I made note of the following.

Turkey is extremely cold in December. McDonald's in Turkey tasted different. Calling cards cost a fortune at the airport. Everybody spoke Turkish. Water was expensive. There was no free water-fountain. There are no carpeted floors to sleep on. And while I am at it, Sabiha Gokchen is not Dubai International Airport.

I was the only non-Turk waiting for the flight. I was the only one wearing sneakers, a t-shirt and shivering in the cold. Everyone else was bundled up in coats, sweaters, head scarves, leather jackets, stockings and boots—all of the same colour—and if I were asked to identify them from a police line-up I would have failed. Everyone stared at me and from their expressions I figured they were judging my lack of foresight.

Pegasus flew over the snow-dusted mountains nudging the Black Sea and every time outlines of human settlement appeared in the cradle of the mountains, my heart missed several beats. If Trabzon was in the nook of those brooding black rocks and Sumela Monastery was somewhere in its folds, I wouldn't leave. I would find work in the monastery and be a monk. Or so, my mind decided midair.

࿇

I'd only been in Trabzon for ten minutes and had only made it down the runway to the exit hall of the airport but I felt like I could stay there forever.

The moment I saw İbrahim looking warm in a jacket, I was committed to my belief in couchsurfing. İbrahim had stepped right out of his Facebook page and I was glad he hadn't been pretending to be someone else and with that washed away any fears I may have had about couchsurfing.

I had a good feeling about this.

Thank You, Casey Fenton.

My first words to him were, 'I am going to stay here forever. I love it already.'

I don't know if that scared him, but he smiled, grabbed my backpack, raised an eyebrow at my lack of warm clothes and directed me to a car.

'Are you cold? Do you have a sweater?'

'No. But I think I will have to get one. It's really cold…brrr.'

The inside of the car was warmer. 'Yes. It is very cold this time of the year. You must get a sweater.'

There was something about the name of the city Trabzon which I loved. I loved the sound of it, I loved saying it and I loved hearing İbrahim say it. He said it with so much love and pride. It had such a musical ring to it. It was perfect for a city built on small, curvy hills overlooking the Black Sea, lined with green trees and Ottoman houses. It looked like a place people were content to live in and never leave.

'Here, this is for you. You might need it,' he handed me a key as soon as we reached his apartment on Kaymakli Street. It was a very functional pad unlike a bachelor's living quarter and my bedroom had the best view of the sea beyond. I sank into the bed for a quick nap.

Boy, it was cold.

An hour later İbrahim knocked on my door.

'Are you hungry?'

'Yes. I think it's the mountain air because I did eat on the flight too. I am hungry, yeah.'

'Let's go eat *hamsi* and buy a coat.'

'Hamsi?'

'Yes. Hamsi. Anchovy in English. It is the best in Trabzon. Very famous. Very delicious. Trabzon is the best place on the entire Black Sea coast for hamsi.'

Hamsi clearly was a much respected fish.

I am a sucker for culinary surprises; in fact, if I don't get one, I plunge into the depths of culinary hell. The food made all the difference. I say a lot of things, but about this I am serious.

So we left on a *dolmuş,* a small bus, to Meydan, the city centre, to savour this delicacy. I followed İbrahim into a restaurant facing the statue of Ataturk. And hell broke loose.

In this hell were tall, well-built, apron-clad Turks with towers of ceramic plates who rapidly closed in on me. I had the feeling of being in a badly made Bollywood movie. They were close enough for me to smell fish on their apron.

Had I put my wrong foot forward? I couldn't have said anything stupid, because I hadn't opened my mouth, except to smile.

Then I heard İbrahim.

'Musafir. Hindustan.'

That I understood. The rest was Turkish.

Then the plates started to fall. Two went straight to the floor at my feet. A saucer followed and then a few dozen spoons. What was it about *a Musafir, Hindustan* (literally, traveller, India) that invited such calculated violence?

When enough destruction was caused, the circle broke up and turned into a line. The men stood respectfully and smiled. I tried.

Then everybody laughed. Then by turns, each of the men grabbed my hands and shook them. After a painful eternity, İbrahim explained.

'This is a tradition. When a visitor you have never seen before, hailing from a country you have only heard of and were not likely to visit, arrives at your doorstep for the very first time it is important to make them feel welcome. Breaking plates is a way to welcome you. It's a tradition.'

I was escorted to a table. Even before I sat down, other diners had whipped out their mobile phones to take pictures of me. I was going to have to smile a lot and exercise patience if I was ever going to get to the hamsi. But first, I had to be the good ambassador for my country they lovingly called Hindustan.

Then finally I met the hamsi, the fish with an envious reputation.

It was small, the size of my finger, plump with a heavy flour coating, arranged neatly on a gleaming white porcelain plate.

From the tenderness with which it was placed on my table, it was clear this finger-length fish ruled the culinary scene in Trabzon. İbrahim smiled every time I reached for the plump, juicy, corn-flour coated anchovies fried to a delicious crisp, mumbling how delicious it was. This was followed by the hamsi-pilaf, hamsi-something and hamsi-something else but I loved every variation of the fish.

The hamsi had a reason to be.

ഗ്ഗ

That evening after buying a coat, İbrahim introduced me to Eren and Sara. Eren Komorlu was a research assistant in the mining engineering department at Karadeniz Technical University, same as İbrahim and Sara Demir, İbrahim's girlfriend who was a PhD student at the university in the landscape department. Except me, ours was a group of intellectuals, but none of that came in between as we sipped Turkish coffee in a second floor café on Long Street or Uzun Sokak, if you prefer the Turkish name.

Eren was a fascinating specimen, the kind of person you wish to have around if marooned, because besides making you laugh, he could read your future in everything, including Turkish coffee cups.

And to prove it he picked up my cup, stared into it and declared, 'You will meet a rich old man. Soon. Rich man, ah, lucky you. You must marry this rich, fat man. He will show you how to eat hamsi and you can live in Trabzon forever.'

Then he cracked a *simit* joke, just like the cops and donut joke, after which we sauntered to Şişman bar for Efes Pilsener, a Trabzon favourite.

It was when we were pushing our way through the evening crowd that I saw a pair of blue leather boots. Okay, I could afford it, but I didn't want to break my self-imposed travel philosophy of not buying expensive stuff I'd have no use for later. I wanted to break the rule, just once. And because I am a stickler for self-imposed rules, I refused to buy it. But you could see I was labouring under the stress of denial.

'Buy it,' İbrahim said.

'To remember Trabzon,' said Eren.

'Girls like boots. You must have it,' said Sara.

'There is no justice in this world,' I moaned. 'How could I?'

Even the combined efforts of Efes Pilsner and Eren couldn't pull me out of the slump I was experiencing at the thought of those boots. I went to bed thinking of it.

The sound of pouring rain woke me up at 4:30 am and if that sounds like a good thing, it's because it was. My first rain in Trabzon. It magically mellowed my thoughts, took it to a faraway place that perhaps did not exist, making me miss something I did not have.

Then somewhere during that half-conscious thought process I fell asleep thinking of Sumela Monastery and somewhere on the fringes of an incoherent dream, the blue boots.

And again, I missed something I did not have. Something to hold me to one place, any place on earth. Even Trabzon.

Breakfast was a cheerful event; I had tea with a light, crunchy, golden brown simit. İbrahim had also introduced me to *kuymak*, a cornmeal mush with loads of butter and on that chilly morning it felt like heaven. For that duration when I slurped the cornmeal mush, even the boots were forgotten.

'It tastes very good with jam,' explained İbrahim picking up the third simit, determined to show me every type of Trabzon food.

'It's great just the way it is,' I said biting into one, in between eating the kuymak. I was on a mission to eat everything that Trabzonians ate for breakfast and in every possible combination but jam was a strict no-no.

In the end and with a little persuasion, I made friends with the bottle of jam. İbrahim was pleased.

'In the evening we buy the boots,' he said as I boarded the tour bus to Sumela Monastery. Damn İbrahim.

ꕥ

The rain was gone and there was some hint of the sun during our short drive through sleepy villages and winding mountain roads leading to the monastery. Parts of the monastery came into view and the prospect of walking to it was exciting. It is another thing that the only walking required of us was a mere two hundred metres which brought us to the monastery's stone walls.

It was on this 'mere stretch of two hundred metres' that I met Irene, a solo Taiwanese backpacker who was as badly winded as I was and quite clueless when it came to the use of the self-mode on her camera. Like me.

We became friends. I later learnt, like me, she couldn't read maps either.

Sumela Monastery perched on the edge of a cliff face in the Altindere National Park made a spectacular sight and it would be a shame to overlook this place if you were in Trabzon. Built high on a cliff, it commanded excellent views of the valley, giving also the adventurous visitors the satisfaction of trekking up to it via a steep and overgrown path.

The story of the monastery's peculiar location will vary depending on whom you speak to. The most popular explanation involves a belief in miracles if you are to accept it as the truth. It starts with two priests and a statue—the Black Madonna. From here the story goes different ways and takes on colourful interpretations and it is really up to you which one you want to believe.

Either way, the monastery functioned peacefully for hundreds of years, till the Turkish war of independence put an end to daily life in the monastery and in 1923, it was abandoned and many items were secretly smuggled to a new monastery in Greece. It is believed that the Black Madonna was one of them.

First, you climb up a flight of stairs, sit yourself on the stones to catch your breath and perhaps take pictures because it has the best views of the inner courtyard, then descend via a rocky stairwell where assorted frescos partially remain after years of abuse by vandals and vain tourists hoping to immortalise their names.

Even if you are not an expert on monasteries, this one in particular will appeal to you, although you are not allowed entry into all parts of it. But the sections you can visit are enough to give you an insight into the life of yore.

On the right were small bedrooms used by the monks. The stone walls projected a cold and stark atmosphere, warmed only by the sun streaming in between the bars of gated windows facing green mountains.

The old kitchens were closed to the public but the highlight of the monastery is the communal church. Intricate and colourful frescoes covering the ceilings and walls deflected from the small size of the room and instead promoted a majestic and silent vibe, only interrupted by the guide shouting at visitors to turn their camera flash off.

The Miracle Well was particularly interesting, although I think you find variations of these in all holy places around the world. It is really simple, but it works—I am not sure why, but it does. The well is actually a deep, stone-lined square into which a very thin stream of water falls from a height, sometimes missing the well if the wind is strong enough to blow it away. The miracle is in one's ability to 'catch' the stream of water!

I am a believer in miracles. I even craned my neck till it hurt just so I could reach the sporadic water drops that flowed from somewhere in the mountains, sure that I would get whatever I had asked for.

However, when we returned to the base, the bus that brought us had left. It didn't help that a group member told me that the more we worried about the cold and hunger, the worse it would be and that we could walk downhill really fast and hope to catch something back to Trabzon. But we found our bus parked by a bubbling stream, had a word with the driver about his negligence before digging into the delicious *cayir lahanasi corbasi* or wild cabbage soup that tastes especially yummy in the cold afternoon.

I found out another thing about Irene. She disliked being called Chinese.

On our quest for Trabzon bread that evening, we bumped into a Turkish woman in a traditional skirt and headscarf, eager for a conversation with us. She threw me a questioning look.

'India, Hindustan,' I offered helpfully.

'Hindustan? Hindustan?'

She repeated it five times, each time with a little more enthusiasm, then grabbed my arm and shook it for a good minute before looking down at my fingers trying to locate a wedding ring.

'No,' I said, shaking my head and making a sad face.

She thumped my chest sharply and said something which Irene interpreted as—

'She says if you have boobs like that, you ought to get yourself a man.'

'You are kidding, aren't you? Really? And how did you figure that one out?'

'Guesswork, of course. Why else would she point at your boobs? This is so funny. Gosh, I could die laughing.'

The woman inspected my uncovered arms, feeling it like a leg of meat. Something about the size of my arms made her smile for she proceeded to pinch my cheeks before pointing back at my empty ring finger and continuing a conversation in Turkish.

'She is telling you to find a man,' Irene translated.

'I will,' I said. I am sure she didn't get that, but she gestured heavenwards with folded hands and said, 'Allah.'

Then she pointed at Irene and said, 'Cheeni,' and ambled away.

Cheeni was the colloquial name for China known only to old-timers who did not keep up with the modern terminology. Like that old cow.

Irene called out after her. 'Taiwan. Taiwan, not China.'

She clearly didn't like being called Chinese. I wouldn't too, if I was Taiwanese, but that is another story.

We continued our quest for the Trabzon bread.

Now I pause a while here and tell you about the Trabzon bread or *Vakfikebir Ekmegi*. This bread, produced in Vakfikebir and Beşikdüzü ranges from 450 gram to 7.5 kilos in weight, is baked in a wood-fired stone oven, and is leavened with natural sour dough. Vakfıkebir bread is full of flavour, has a long shelf life, and does not mould easily. It is considered good even when it goes stale. Such is the Trabzon bread and given its vibrant profile, who could have walked away from it without first being introduced to it?

Not us. We found it and photographed it. Later we wandered towards the sea, sipping *ayran,* a yoghurt-based drink, and accepting every offer of free tea for foreign tourists. Ayran was similar in taste to the *laban* in UAE and the salted *lassi* so common in India.

The rocks by the sea and the area around it also happened to be the city's corner for love-struck graffiti artists, or so it seemed going by the many declarations of *Seni Seviyorum* in multicolours enclosed in ill-shaped hearts, some with arrows going through them as well.

The next morning Irene and I took a self-guided tour of the city, managing rather well in a place that spoke little English. İbrahim had given us a piece of paper with directions in English and Turkish, so that helped. It was not really that difficult to find the Ataturk Museum or the Hagia Sophia so we agreed that guidebooks were really cumbersome and handwritten notes were the best way to get about.

Later that evening, Irene had her fortune told by Eren in a coffee shop in Boztepe. He said she would meet a 'fat, old man' and live in Trabzon forever.

I wondered if that was wishful thinking because Irene left the next day for Şanliurfa not giving enough time for his predictions to come true.

ꕥ

I would be leaving too, in two days, but I wanted to live there forever, trying out different pubs, listening to live music that changed every few feet, drinking Efes with the guys. There was something about Trabzon—the way the rain fell, creating a magic that can't be explained, the way the rainwater pooled in the brick streets. The sidewalks full of people drinking sweet tea out of minuscule tea cups, delicious simits full of sesame seeds, the smiling shoe shiners, the heavily dressed people with their hands in their pockets, the fish displayed in front of every restaurant, the smell of anchovies, the dolmuş…

I wanted to know which pub sold the crispiest fish and chips, which coffee shop made the best coffee, which bands played where each night. I wanted to know those secluded spots to escape to, where to wander when I needed fresh air to clear my head. I wanted to meet people to share stories and dance with without a care…

I get that way when I reach a new place, sometimes. There is so much to explore that I am overwhelmed. I want to know it all, see it all, and experience it all. I want to find things about it the average person doesn't know. I imagined my life there.

I wanted to know Trabzon like that.

When I boarded the bus to Göreme/Nevsehir two days later, I cried. I watched Eren and İbrahim fade as the bus pulled away. I should have pinched İbrahim's t-shirt. To feel İbrahim through it. Something to connect me to him and Trabzon.

Yes. I loved Trabzon like that.

ꕥ

And it rained.

The mercury levels dipped to a new low, going from being comfortably cold to uncomfortably freezing. Rains were great but on a December night in one of Turkey's colder regions, it opened up certain eventualities I didn't quite like to think about. It meant a substantial investment in warm clothes. I had already spent a considerable sum on the blue leather boots darn, Turkey was expensive, it was.

But the second worry was that I had not called Cetin, the guy who three weeks ago had promised me a free room in a cave in Göreme. I should have called. If he refused, I would have a lot more to deal with than just the cold.

Cetin had seemed eager three weeks ago; maybe I could just surprise him? What if he refused? Turks were rather cool sort of people, true that, but…

Fortunately I slept through the night and when I arrived in the Flinstone-landscape the following morning, it had stopped raining, but the temperature remained floored. With newfound optimism, I hoofed it to Sunset Cave Hotel to surprise Cetin.

That evening, as the cold winds blew down the grey-and-white penis-shaped rocks and stars shone bright in the clear night skies, Cetin Chico and I drank cold beer on the cave terrace like old friends, discussing Dubai, Turkey and tourism. How similar we all were, especially after a few bottles because it had pretty much the same effect on our senses. We sang.

A CAVE OF HAIR

In Avanos the next morning, I devised my own tongue-twister to keep me amused.

Pretty Pottery Town I called it. Repeating it in succession was amusing. Pretty because on the day of my arrival Avanos looked as though it had woken up from a peaceful slumber on a wintery morning and was content to be just a town on the banks of the Kizilirmak (Red River) full of lazy ducks—that and nothing else.

There wasn't a lot to show for its remote past but Pretty Pottery Town was filled with reminders of the nineteenth and early twentieth centuries when it had a large Greek and Armenian population. You could see that in the many beautiful old stone houses whose façades were far more elaborately decorated than those of nearby Göreme, with wonderful window carvings and long bands of deep relief separating the ground and first floors.

It was pretty all right. Plus, the big urns added a touch of quaintness.

There are two ways to reach Avanos. If you were in Göreme, you could catch a bus there and backtrack to Avanos. A few old buses ran this route few times in a day but if you were arriving here from Nevsehir or Kayşeri and going towards Göreme as most people do, you could get off at Avanos. I had passed this town on the way to Göreme without alighting.

If you were driven by curiosity then all that pottery lying about would be your cue to alight here. Avanos is surrounded by a horde of tourist attractions and pottery but one doesn't come to Avanos for the caves or the Red River, although one might be coaxed into coming for the pottery. But that could be my impression.

I was here for the other thing—the secret that Avanos has guarded so well. Okay, maybe I am dramatising a little here because the secret of Avanos I mention has made it to the *Guinness Book of World Records* but you can forgive me for being a little dramatic.

It was that secret I had come to see. Turning my attention towards a cave that had been called spooky, weird and even scary, I walked briskly through the cobbled streets past the bus-stop and the big statue of a potter smiling at the mugs and pitchers, and made my way past various Turkish coffee pots scattered about the town.

Weird, definitely weird, not spooky, I told myself. A cave could not be spooky unless there were ghosts living it. Could there be ghosts in the cave in Avanos?

The walk had been short and brisk. I arrived at the door of *Chez Galip* which operates in the officially designated Avanos Çanakçilar Bölgesi (Avanos Pottery Zone) to the east of town and smiled at a young man in dirty jeans who was lounging about the door.

'Welcome to the cave,' said he. 'You are the first customer to come this way today. Welcome.'

That was the best conversation starter I had ever come across.

'Hello, hello, this is the Hair Museum, correct?'

Of course it was. I was standing under the board that announced it. Still, it was a good ice-breaker.

'Yes, yes, come in. Welcome, it is very cold today. Sit down, please.'

I sat. But because I couldn't keep quiet, I launched straight into a conversation.

'I am here to meet Mr Galip. Can you tell me where I can find him?'

The young man did not answer right away. Instead he wandered to the back of the cave and straightened a few pieces of pottery lying about. While waiting for my question to be answered, I let my eyes sweep over the cave walls towards the rows of fragile and colourful pottery in the dim light, admiring the intricate pottery, afraid that in some way I would break everything to bits just by looking at them and end up slaving for years to cover the loss.

Something about the dimly lit interiors and gaping holes in the cave walls made me panic.

I had experienced a similar but a slightly stronger panic attack in the Underground City of Derinkuyu the previous day and just looking at the labyrinth of rock-cut rooms filled with expensive ceramic was causing my head to spin and make my breath come in laboured gasps.

I couldn't understand it.

Did the women really come into this panic-inducing cave just to donate a lock of their hair that kind of made them immortal? Was that why I was here too? Would I survive it?

The young man returned with bad news. 'Mr Galip does not come every day. Today, he do not come. I show you pottery and Hair Museum. Come with me.'

My earlier panic returned.

The idea of coming to a lesser-known town and to put myself into a cave that about fifty thousand women around the world had visited at one time or the other seemed spooky. Could I actually find the courage to go into the Bluebeard's den?

I hesitated. The young man sat himself in front of me.

'I am his nephew,' said he. 'My name is Ahmet. Would you like to look at pottery? Good discount. First customer.'

I was the first customer all right—it was early and cold and not to mention that it was the low season. But insistent pottery-sellers are worse than the mythical snakes guarding the treasure cave, except that they can be charmed into changing their minds.

'Yes, of course,' I began in what was the perfect start of evasion. 'I see some amazing stuff here. But tell me about the hair museum. I have come all the way from Dubai to donate my lock of hair.'

'You will first drink tea, yes? Apple tea? Yes?'

Yes, of course. In Turkey when someone offered you tea, it was polite to accept it. Tea never harmed anyone. Tea and good conversation were the fuel that kept the tourism dollars flowing throughout Turkey.

I accepted a cup. With two cubes of sugar.

Tea in hand, the conversation began. We talked about where I've been in Turkey and if I liked what I saw, especially the Fairy Chimneys.

I got down to specifics.

'These cups and plates and urns must be expensive, right? How much do they cost anyway?'

'Yes. Very expensive. See that? That one…'

I squinted. Ahmet, like the true artist-turned-salesman that he was, expertly picked up a saucer and brought it over. 'This is Hittite art.'

That didn't explain much so I kept my curiosity and patience alive by raising a brow.

'They are very intricate designs. Takes a lot of time and patience and experience. My uncle is the best here. He makes the best Hittite art.'

A series of pictographs in cuneiform script perhaps told a story in the BC, but that was Hittite art. Older than Jesus Christ and at the risk of sounding very stupid indeed, I said the first thing that came to my mind.

Ahmet pressed another cup as he continued to explain the process of pottery designing and suggested a tour of the cave only after I finished the third cup.

I followed him through various cave rooms filled with beautiful and fragile pottery waiting to be admired or possessed but my mind was not seeing them.

Ahmet paused at a very narrow entrance to what seemed like the way to a dimly lit interrogation chamber and signalled me upwards. It was bad enough that a visit to the Derinkuyu had proved I suffered from claustrophobia I didn't know I had, but to find myself facing a narrow opening in a cave once again was doing bad things to my bladder full of apple tea.

I hesitated.

'Come on, follow me,' Ahmet's voice floated down the narrow passage. He had somehow disappeared inside while I was staring at the entrance unsure of what to do.

It was now or never. I had to take the plunge.

I coughed a little, trying to ignore the panic attack, telling myself that beating claustrophobia was the only way to become an immortal part of the hair-donating brigade.

I closed my eyes to slits and took the first step.

An eternity of walking in a stoop through the cold, damp cave later I stepped inside Galip's Scary Chamber.

There was hair everywhere. Pale yellow light from the low-watt bulbs made the cave smaller than it was and spookier somehow. Inside the cold, yellow cave I started to sweat. To distract myself, I whipped out a camera and was about to photograph an inch of hair when Ahmet interjected.

'No pictures here please.'

'Huh?'

Photography, it seemed, was not encouraged for reasons of protecting the identity of thousands of women who had 'donated' their lock of hair and left behind their addresses on pieces of paper on which hair was glued before being stuck on the walls.

I did manage to get a photograph, of course, but it was only after we returned to the main cave, had more tea, and sealed the deal on a few items of pottery that set me back fifty dollars. I had to make a trip through the narrow, claustrophobic cave just to get a few pictures.

I met a different Ahmet when waiting for the bus to Göreme. This Ahmet had a car and was driving up to Göreme and didn't mind giving me a lift.

'First we visit my uncle's shop and see pottery. We drink tea.'

This, I realised, was to trick me into buying something under the guise of meeting 'my uncle'. Tea could have been the bait. Or free transport. But what tickled me was that Avanos was full of Ahmets whose uncles were in the business of pottery.

Ahmet was a man with a dream. He wanted to go to USA because he was tired of seeing the caves in Göreme. Well, it was a good enough reason, one that wasn't controversial, so I said nothing. As long as I had him showing me the valleys of Cappadocia for free, I was ready to laud his decisions on anything. He led me through the Pigeon Valley with its long trail of promising sights of manmade caves and told me interesting stories about how the birds nested in these holes once upon a time and their droppings were used by the people to fertilise their lands.

It was really weird how slap bang in the middle of a countryside, you find churches cut into rocks and adorned with frescoes, underground cities and caves where people once lived.

Walking through valleys full of penis-shaped rocks was one thing, but to actually imagine living inside one of them was quite another. The wind, weather and water had done a good job of chiselling the canyons into bizarre phallic-shaped rocks and funnily enough, there was an entire valley with rocks shaped like various animals, a valley that was entirely made up of pinkish rocks, another was fully white and when you walked through these valleys, you got the impression that you had wandered into a movie set that pretended to be on the moon.

ꕤ

I did not see Cetin that night, which was a little strange, and hence I decided to leave Göreme and head to Pamukkale the next day. Fortunately I did not have a plan so it really hadn't mattered where I went. Ahmet, who had been expecting more than a hug at the end of the valley tour, didn't show any further interest in showing me the secrets of Göreme, and I had pretty much had my fill of pottery and caves. I booked a seat on a bus to Pamukkale without visiting Kayseri as I had promised my friend.

Kayseri was of no real value to the tourist. My reasons to go to Kayseri were different. I had promised a friend, who had spent twenty-eight months of her life in Kayseri as a refugee from Iran before Australia granted her asylum, that I would bring her a picture of the mosque where she had spent a considerable amount of time pondering over her future, but I couldn't make it back to Kayseri.

I hoped she would understand.

ꕤ

I am going to run through Pamukkale for the only reason that I was being a tourist doing the typical rounds of the famed travertines and Roman ruins, drinking tea and wandering through Karahayit and bathing in hot water springs and not much else. I would have been just as happy doing none of those, too, for the weather was perfect and I liked walking through the narrow streets that snaked around small hills with houses built close to each other and eating fruits from the branches bending over the compound walls. I had so far met three Turks with the name Ahmet and the fourth was in Pamukkale with whom I drank the legendary Pamukkale wine and who later suggested going to his place for more—an offer I refused because I was far too drunk anyway.

Thank heavens, I wasn't couching with him.

But what I will bring up is the buying of towels in Denizli and eating *manti*, a popular meat dumpling served with sour cream that came highly recommended by Najla, the friend I mentioned earlier. The ever-smiling Najla had made me swear that I would eat manti and not wanting to disappoint her the second time, I accompanied Ahmet of the earlier evening to Denizli to check out towels and onyx and perhaps feed on manti.

Towels? Yes. It may not be a major touristic draw, but it is true that Denizli is renowned for its towels as much as its onyx and travertines. I bought six of varying sizes but that morning at the huge Varol Textile I was the one with the least purchase. Scandinavian women touring this side of Turkey bought everything they could lay their hands on. I had never seen a towel market of this scale before and to see men and women grab towels like that was mildly amusing. Well, what do you know? Clearly there were lots of people with a towel fetish.

Later, when I had gotten over the shock of seeing towels disappear off the shelves, I ate manti to appease my mind. Only then I realised why Najla had insisted that I give it a shot. It is comfort food, easily found, wholesome and not expensive if you are on a budget, but you should try it just because it is great. Everyone eats manti. I should have liked it with a glass of apple wine that I was getting addicted to.

In hindsight I wished I had some more time to explore the cave in the region—a cave with a waterfall, according to Ahmet. But it was not to be, so along with the cave-with-the-waterfall, some old ruins, like that of Heiropolis, remained unexplored, because I had to leave.

For practical reasons, I do not buy anything that will not fit into my backpack but in Denizli, along with towels, I bought eggplant skins. Let me explain. While walking through Karahayit, I came upon a local woman with a cart full of spices and eggplant skins dangling on a branch above. At first, I didn't place the shrivelled, purplish cone but looking closely, I realised this was the skin I had eaten rice out of somewhere in Göreme. I bought a string of this from her, because I spent a considerable amount of time at her cart admiring the shells of dried pepper and drinking some of her tea because she was a keen conversationalist despite not speaking a word of English, except 'English, No.'

I hoped, that some day back home, I would treat myself to some Turkish food, namely eggplant *dolma* that had tasted so good in Göreme. For the recipe, there was Google. Hence the skin. It was not heavy but every time I put down the backpack, I feared I would break the sun-dried cone and miss out on the chance of learning to make dolma. That kept me on my toes till I decided to give it away.

That night at the bus station of Denizli, when waiting for the bus for Istanbul, I met Nuntaporn and Tui Rsw, friends and travel partners from Thailand who were vacationing in Turkey during their annual leave.

We became friends. My yearning for the company of English-speaking people was so strong that I invited myself into their group by offering to buy tea and then insisted on tagging along till we'd reached Istanbul and maybe after that as well. They were good girls, they were travelling with typical Thai-style suitcases with lots of bling.

We had separate seats on the bus, of course, mine being the worst due to a last-minute booking, but I am not the complaining kind. I could sleep on a bucking bronco for all I cared.

When we reached Istanbul, nine hours later, I was glad I had tagged along with the girls. I am not sure how I would have explained to anyone at the bus station that I needed to find a dorm without pulling out my hair.

The girls and I grabbed simits from a cart and hoofed it to their hostel, which, at seven euros, was reasonably cheap and comfortable.

Turkey wasn't the sort of place that allowed you to enjoy isolation very much and bored you quickly, especially when you didn't have the luxury of meeting fellow backpackers. Ironical because I like a lot of me-time but my outlook improved right after befriending them.

I had many interesting stories on Thailand to share with them too.

SAFAK DENIZ AND THE PRICE OF PRIDE

Istanbul turned me into a tourist.

Hurriedly munching sandwiches, Tui, Nuntaporn and I boarded the tram headed for the Bosphorus and landed amidst a sea of touts hawking cheap tickets for the cruise. The cold had kept away the rational traveller from rocking over the Bosphorus, but as the newest member of the typical-tourist-clan I behaved exactly like them, trying to cram everything into one microscopic itinerary because 'I wanted to see and do it all' not really caring if it was going to freeze me to death.

'Everything is so grey,' Tui lamented pulling her jacket closer. 'Why it is so cold today? I want tea. Brrrrrrr, I wish the sun would come out. It is never so cold in Thailand. I miss home.'

The city was indeed grey, from the skies to the churning waters and everything in between, including the people, the quay and the buildings, everything was covered in variations of grey so that one actually appreciated the cunning of grey in transforming into so many different shades of its own colour.

Expectedly, the boat was only partially full and before we set sail, the three of us had become friends with the two other girls dressed up in heavy winter clothes and when we had completed about a tenth of the tour, we knew everything there was to know about each others' jobs, marital status and take on men.

Tesse Brunke, a German with pale blue eyes and soft brown hair and Ayse Deschanel, a German of Turkish origin, were friends and colleagues who worked at Disney in Munich. But as conversation progressed, I realised that girls everywhere followed a pattern when it came to men, shopping and describing the weather and to my disbelief, I realised how much of 'the girl' I had become in a shockingly short time. It was fun too, really, because it was always so different with the guys—I never complained about anything. But girls, they understood cribbing.

Our being single was the final bond and although I have no idea what that said about us or the men of the world, it was comforting to know single women world over enjoyed travelling and still wished to run into their Prince along the way. I didn't have a boyfriend yet and being single was the quickest way to find a common ground.

In a male group it was the only thing to say anyway.

My nose by this time had started to peel. But then, it peels in summer. It peels in winter. But between the two seasons it does look somewhat new. That, however, is not the point I want to make—what I want to say is that when it peels, it makes a ghastly sight. Like now.

Tesse offered me a cream.

'You look weird with your nose like that,' was her observation. The others agreed. That was the thing about girls. They had one opinion on everything.

'You will look funny in your pictures, you don't want that!'

There were, on the cruise, a few unconnected males and a very pregnant woman with a peculiar affinity for the cold, who did not fear climbing metal stairs on a violently lurching boat merely to sit on the freezing deck.

'I don't care if you judge me, but that is positively creepy,' said Tesse pointing at the retreating back of the pregnant woman. It could have been her German accent but she seemed pretty shook up.

'What is she thinking?'

Not the one to remain quiet, I threw in my bit.

'She is probably going to give birth to an icicle,' said I and that sort of ended that conversation.

Everyone agreed.

'Let's hang out,' Ayse suggested. 'We could go to Taksim for drinks later tonight? How about that?'

Everyone agreed.

We were a determined bunch of Thais, Germans and an Indian looking forward to enjoying a little girl time. But Tesse laid down the rules. I think it was the German foresight.

'If two or more of us are interested in the same guy, we have to be polite. Let the first one take lead,' she said seriously. 'We must not ruin someone's chances.'

Everyone agreed.

Then we made a mistake. We decided to run through the Grand Bazaar first. But then all of us had been in agreement over the Grand Bazaar tour.

We were girls like that.

Grand Bazaar is the place where the world congregates when looking for Turkish souvenirs. It is not a bazaar built on a flat ground; it is a series of misleading alleys running up and down a series of elevated surfaces requiring the shopper to walk in every direction before figuring out that they are lost in the maze of coloured glass and lights. It is the most confusing shopping spree I have ever been on because I kept seeing the same things over and over again and didn't understand why the girls insisted on picking up every single item on display, bargaining and walking away gleefully without making a purchase.

When you have spent an afternoon shivering on a ship, walked through this maze of useless curios, exerted your lungs screaming over the din, you do tend to feel a little breathless. I am not used to hurrying. I do not care about having seen *everything* in one place. I believe in taking things slow, absorbing the essence of local life and damn if I didn't see 'it all'.

You get my drift.

This pointless flitting about in Grand Bazaar was not amusing. If I had a choice, I'd have happily avoided it for the lack of time. Being a tourist with limited time really sucked! It put so much demand on your body's constitution and pressurised your mind into doing things in ways you did not want to. At this point I wanted to give up the whirlwind tour and just be a backpacker.

And I was tired.

'Let's just get to Taksim early? I am sure we have had enough shopping for today?'

Tui and Nuntaporn agreed.

'I love it here,' said Tessa. 'I love this market. I want to buy everything!'

But Tessa had not purchased anything yet and we had already been in the bazaar for over three hours.

'I have a feeling that if we don't leave now, we might regret the traffic. I heard it can be bad.'

In reality, I had heard no such thing, but I had only drawn an obvious conclusion. Taksim was Istanbul's hub of night life and saw more traffic and people during the night, although some travellers have called it a big ugly square full of watering holes and a park.

Everyone saw sense in that. When we appeared at the exit, it was raining. Ayse had a suggestion.

'I am going to run that way and try to get a cab. You guys run when I wave. There is no reason why all of us should get wet in this blasted rain.'

With that, she ran into the rain. Tessa took off after her, followed by Tui and Nuntaporn. I watched them go.

In the blink of an eye, the ocean of black coats swept them away and out of sight. I stopped where I was and stared into the dim light and falling rain. They were gone. I did not run after them, knowing it to be a useless exercise.

Now, if you have been in Istanbul in winter, you will see that it was not my fault. People here dress alike—in heavy, black, ankle-length coats with hoodies pulled over their heads which understandably makes it hard for the watcher to tell the person's gender, nationality or otherwise. I had been staring at the backs of such black-coated people in the dim lights. What were my chances I would identify Tesse and Ayse in the ocean?

So I had returned to the dorm, cold, wet and miserable, but strangely relieved. The temperature had plunged some time during the evening, but when I walked into the heated dormitory, I was ready to collapse. The dorm felt like heaven. All my dorm mates were out. I wanted tea.

But the sight of my bed put an end to my desire for tea.

'I must write a positive review of this hostel, I should,' I told myself opening the wardrobe to hang up my coat. 'I love this place. I will, too, when I get back. One more day…sigh, two more cold and rainy days…'

I missed the December sun of Dubai.

Those were my last wistful thoughts before I turned into someone else.

ᢀ

In the wardrobe I found a coat hanger. *And on it was the most beautiful fawn-coloured coat I had ever seen.*

Some instinct urged me to touch it. The moment I did, I wanted it.

A simple, yet insanely powerful desire for a stranger's belonging.

'No,' I told myself. 'What you are thinking of, is not an option. People don't pinch stuff. Plus, I don't need another coat, do I? What the hell am I thinking?'

I continued a very moralistic conversation with myself.

'Shut the door. Forget the coat. You do not need another—of course not—most certainly NOT. Stop being ridiculous. You are being greedy. Let it go.'

I lost the argument with myself. I slipped it on.

There was no faulting it. The texture, the style, the colour, the fit—everything was perfect. It was soft. And warm. It was what one wished to have in Istanbul's cold weather—stylish and warm. It carried a label.

It had been made with me in mind.

Suddenly I was envious of the unknown owner. No, the feeling was deeper than mere envy. I hated her. Even as I chewed on an early dinner, I thought of the coat. It was beautiful.

I wanted it.

ꙮ

I don't recall the time Tui and Nuntaporn returned—I think around midnight. They looked tired but relieved.

'We thought you got lost. Are you all right?'

'Yes, oh yes, I am all right. You guys just vanished. I swear I looked. Everyone there looked the same. Gosh, I hope you guys had a good time. Did you miss me at all?'

'Yes and no. You should have been there; we got bored after a while. Not much drinking and definitely no flirting or anything. How boring.'

I was glad to hear they missed me. It flattered my ego. Unless they meant that it would have been easier to hook a guy with me around because I was sort of an expert at starting conversations with strangers, especially men.

'We will leave early in the morning. So we say goodbye now.'

We exchanged email addresses, phone numbers and hugs and sometime later when they went into the shower, I slept again. I never saw them after that. I woke up to their empty beds and felt a tinge of sadness. They were such great gals, really.

ꕥ

When I woke up the memory of the coat had vanished and my mind had switched to the most important reason of my being in Istanbul.

My agenda for the day was one of a literary nature. I was eager to visit a particular museum that was full of stuff a relentless hoarder or an obsessed lover would display as a mark of his obsession with a woman. The Museum of Innocence, a museum funded by Orhan Pamuk, the Nobel prize winner for literature, who had sunk his prize money into a three-storeyed museum, consisted entirely of artifacts he collected through his life which eventually featured prominently in his eponymous novel.

I don't have the mindset or fine taste in literature to read through a 500-page book that won him the big prize but I was a hoarder too, though not on the same scale as Orhan Pamuk's creation. What he had created was a work of art and people paid good money to see that work of art.

That was what I wanted to see. The quest for the museum was threatened by the fact that no one I asked knew of its existence. There may have been another way to pronounce Çukurcuma, but I didn't know that.

Thoughtfully, I looked outside the window wondering how, if ever, I was going to get there in the cold and rain. Getting to the museum was going to present challenges I could not fathom and, under the circumstances, face up to. I was okay with the cold and the rain, but to leave the warmth of the dormitory was proving hard.

Then she walked in.

I mean, what kind of a coincidence was that that brought you face to face with the beautiful fawn-colour coat gliding into the room with a woman concealed in it? What the night had done, the morning had undone. The desire came back.

In all honesty I thought the coat didn't belong to her. I mean, it simply could not have been hers. I don't know what it was about that coat and my obsession with it, but it was there. I could not deny it. This coat was making me behave strangely.

My coat-obsessed mind continued to observe. The coat was definitely not hers. It was beautiful and sagged at her shoulders; the upturned collar covered her face, making her look much smaller and uncomfortable. She did not belong in it.

Had she pinched it?

'Hello,' said she gathering up her coat before settling down on the bed.

'Uh - oh - oh - hi.'

I found it hard to look at her with the coat clouding my vision. With a mere five-feet-one-inch frame she had no business to be in a coat that was obviously too big for her.

'Nice coat.'

'Thank you.'

There wasn't a lot I could say after this. We exchanged names.

Safak Deniz was a local. She was in the dorm because she had been too tired to travel home in the Asian side of Istanbul the previous night.

'What about you?'

'Oh, me, I am leaving tonight. But right now, I have to get to Taksim or thereabouts, but I can't be sure. I have to visit the Museum of Innocence.'

My traveller's mask was in place. But my mind continued to lust after the coat.

'Museum? Istanbul is full of them. Which one?'

Safak Deniz spoke a fair amount of English but her knowledge of the local attractions was lacking.

Museums are not in your league, I thought unkindly. Of course, you wouldn't know.

'Museum of Innocence, you know, the one built by Orhan Pamuk, the writer?'

If there was anyone who could help me it was her. She had shown a certain eagerness when talking to me. I hadn't planned on knocking on all the doors in Taksim asking for directions, but I had to get to the museum. I held out the notebook with the address. She stared at it uncertainly and silently.

'Perhaps we could call them first?' I suggested.

'Yes, we could, only it's too early. But I might be able to help you find it. I am going to Taksim too. Come with me.'

I resented her logic but getting her help was important. We stepped out into the drizzle. Istanbul was frozen grey. Safak walked ahead of me on the narrow sidewalk and I couldn't help but stare at the way the coat almost reached her ankle. Her faded brown leather boots did not go well with the coat. I couldn't imagine her walking into a Benetton store in those boots to buy a coat three sizes too large. It could not have happened that way. Something was not right.

All the way to the other side of the Bosphorus and up the funicular to Taksim, I held back the urge to ask her about the coat. I had to know. It bothered me.

The rain continued to fall and the mercury dipped. That bothered me. I was afraid of ruining the new leather boots I purchased in Trabzon two weeks ago. Every time I stepped into a puddle, I hated the city and the rains. Safak was unmindful of the rain falling on her coat and that bothered me.

We walked and we talked. She was touching fifty, single and without a job. And the casual way in which she said that bothered me even more.

'Where is home?'

'Oh, I don't have one. No job and no home. Rented out my father's flat for the money. But otherwise, I have nothing.'

'What? Oh dear, where have you been staying all this while? Surely not at Cordial House?'

'Here and there. When I had a job, I had a room. Now no job, no room. Dorm is cheap, only what I can afford right now.'

With that she pulled out a cigarette and lit up. A casual, elaborate shrug followed.

That bothered me too.

I had to stop myself from getting preachy about smoking. Save the darned money, I wanted to tell her although it was none of my business. Over the last cup of tea, I had begun to think of her as a desperate woman. Desperate, but quite foolish and I insisted on paying for every cup of tea we had together.

Had someone given her that coat? It was a possibility.

I put my arm around her as we walked, shielding her under the cheap umbrella bought from a street vendor. The coat was damp from the rain but she didn't feel it. Or she would have said so. Safak did not believe in niceties.

We found the museum. She waited while I surveyed the interiors. I did not volunteer to pay the twenty-five lira for her and she did not seem interested in any way. Nobel prizes meant nothing to her, she preferred to chat up the receptionist and linger around the heater. Later, we pottered around looking for antique trinkets and beaten-in coffee cups, the collection of which was my current hobby. Safak didn't share my enthusiasm. She liked things 'in the present, antiques were a thing of the past—old' and puffed away on her cigarettes indifferently.

'Hey, let's go shopping,' I suggested breezily. 'No way am I leaving Beyoglu without it. Ha. Come, everything is on sale too—*indirim*, isn't that the word? Come let's find a coat for me—like yours.'

But first, Safak wanted to call someone. We found a local telephone booth where she used a telephone card to make her call.

I didn't ask her what it was about, but whatever it was, wasn't good. Her face hardened, but it could have been the cold. I could not tell.

'Let's go. It's good to be with you. It's a good change.'

She lit another cigarette. The grey smoke rings disappeared in the frozen grey of the old, cobbled city. Suddenly everything felt sinister. Odd. Unreal. And in the midst of it all was Safak—hard and uncaring.

I wanted a coat more than ever.

Every store on Beyoglu, Taksim was on sale. Safak chatted through my repeated attempts at finding the right coat. And I, on my part, didn't really care what she was talking about so long as her chatter was just a constant hum in the background that didn't break the line of my thoughts focused on finding the right coat. A coat better than the fawn-coloured coat she had. Her coat was the benchmark of fine coats.

Safak devised a productive way to occupy her every time I ran into a store on sale. She wandered into every store that advertised a vacancy. Coffee shops, bakeries or shoe stores—nothing deterred her. She wanted a job; anything that could keep her financial machinery rolling. I never asked what transpired at the end of the walk-in-interviews. Aging ex-baby sitters and bank clerks did not fit the description of the candidates people advertised for. Or so her expressions explained.

At some point Safak's expression permanently changed to depression and I lost every interest in coats. The moment of obsession had safely passed. It was getting colder and I wanted to be back in the dorm, eat roasted chestnuts and drink tea.

We stepped out of the last store onto the sidewalk. The rain had not stopped falling. It was cold.

Safak fixed me with a faraway look.

'I know how much you want a coat. I will give you mine. It is not even my size, if you've noticed. You can have it for a hundred. It's a Benetton, very expensive, but you can take it for a hundred.'

The cold got worse. But this time I felt it in my knees, my heart, my mind and my tongue too, for I could not speak. I blurted out incoherently.

'No...I mean, of course, NOT. It's yours, I mean, you need it. I couldn't take it—no, it's very cold, freezing really...' and as a last, desperate attempt to discourage her I finished with an 'I wouldn't fit into it...err, I...'

Lies. Lies. Lies. The coat was a perfect fit. I knew that.

I shivered. The lust bubble popped. I never wanted to see her coat again. Nor her.

Never. Never. Never.

Safak took off her coat and handed it to me.

I hoped it would not fit me. Somehow. It was the only way I could get out of buying a coat I no longer wanted. How could I tell her I didn't want another as long as I lived? Would she think me snooty if I refused? Was there some way to convince her to change her mind?

I slipped it on without a word.

Safak broke in confidently.

'It's perfect. Made for you. I can buy a cheaper one. You know, I have no money but I need the money for cigarettes, for tea, for the dorm.' She patted my arm.

There was no regret in her voice. She had made a practical decision but she had not taken the extreme weather into consideration. The cold could go to hell, but cigarettes and tea—she needed those. And a bed in the dorm.

'I could give you the money instead. Keep the coat.'

'No. I am selling my coat, Anjaly. Right now that is all I have.'

I remembered she had no mobile phone. Had she sold that to someone too?

In the back lanes of Beyoglu were small stores selling cheap coats. They didn't match up to the quality of the branded ones, but people who could not afford the high price were content with these purchases.

Safak was.

Her thirty-two lira coat barely reached her waist. But she was happy and warm, she claimed. I couldn't refute that in any way.

She counted out the balance. 'Sixty-eight liras…three days in the dorm and I will not have to starve either.'

She then handed over the coat. My coat. The deal had gone through easily. What a lot money could do?

I grabbed the coat, eager to hold it, to touch it, to feel it—the pride of ownership, perhaps. I eagerly pressed it against my cheeks. It needed care, of course, but I would see to that at once.

Safak offered to carry it for me, but I refused. My mind had worked up a probable event—what if she disappeared in the crowd with it? The street was crowded. My logic was simple—if I could carry a backpack and an umbrella, I could carry my coat.

We returned to the dorm late in the evening. The mercury was hovering around zero but inside the dorm one tended to forget the outside world. I slipped off my coat and stretched out on the bed.

It had been a good day, although wet and very cold. And I had two coats both of which I would never wear once I left Istanbul a few hours later. I carefully packed them into my backpack while Safak continued to speak.

I watched her as she slipped out of her new coat. I had spent exactly eleven hours in her company and in another hour I would leave. Her name would go into my book as another stranger I met on one of my travels. What was she saying about a job? Something about an interview at the coffee shop? Or was she speaking about her sister who no more spoke to her? Safak had the habit of jumping from one topic to another rather quickly.

Her coat came off. She had a black-and-white sweater under it. Pretty, I thought, pretty, but well used.

'It's rather warm in here,' she said, more to herself than to me. 'I am going to take off this sweater too.'

I continued to watch. Safak removed the sweater. The woollen cap came off with it. Her grey hair was cut very short. With the cap gone, the lines on her face and forehead were more pronounced. She looked every bit of her fifty years. She wore no earrings. No watch. Not even a chain.

She turned to her bed.

Through the large holes in her frayed thermals, I saw the old, white, wrinkled skin on her back, the outline of her underwear with its frayed edges, the skin sagging under the flimsy layer.

How had I missed being human?

Safak Deniz changed the course of my travel. And me.

WITHOUT A CLUE OR A FORK

When I first considered China for a holiday, I was quite unsure of what I had in mind. The stumbling blocks had appeared as soon as I spread the map of China over my table to study its geography.

In the art of learning languages, I am easily beaten. But in self praise, I can say *thank you* in twelve languages, including Khmer. A language was easy to master if and only if I was humming it and I follow this up with an example of that extremely popular Swahili song 'Malaika' that got copied into a Bollywood song and given the nature of its tune, I learnt it easily. I was at an impressionable age of seven then so let it be known that I am not a complete moron. Years may have made me less smart, but I have relied on Bollywood to help me through this linguistic impediment. So before going to China, I looked for a Mandarin song that had inspired Bollywood.

There was none.

I was going to have to deal with my lack of linguistic skills in some other way. Mandarin was a tough one to master. The fact that genius copycats of the Bollywood music industry hadn't bothered with it should have been my first clue, but we will pass over my inability to decipher life's subtle clues, and in keeping with my tradition of following whims, I booked a ticket to Guangzhou, China.

On the map, Guangzhou was a tiny dot in the extreme south and anything I intended to see, like the Great Wall, was straight up north, thousands of kilometres away. China's geographical size was the second clue that I had done something wrong; the third was my decision to fly to Guangzhou when everything I knew about China was elsewhere.

Seeing 'all of China' in three weeks was proving to be a myth and would remain so unless I scored free domestic flights to go everywhere. This brought up another question—would couchsurfing work here? Remember how I was extremely successful with this in Turkey?

After scouring Google I realised that everything I wanted to see was in different directions, for Guangzhou was like the human heart that everything ended at or branched out from. I was not sure that a trek through Tiger Leaping Gorge in Yunnan, a visit to Tianmen Mountains in Hunan and Panda cuddling in Chengdu could be undertaken on a three-week trip. Where did the Great Wall fit in? Or the Shaolin Temple? Or rolling in the meadows at Shangri La?

I reconsidered couchsurfing. Yes, love for uncertainty is a cruel thing as is the hankering for free stays.

Guangzhou was one place I was sure of arriving at because the Chinese humour did not see it fit to sneak the plane elsewhere without first making it national news. If I could find a host in Guanghzou, planning the rest of my trip would be a breeze, but first I had to find out whether China was 'up there in the freebie-stay circle' after having cut out Facebook, Youtube and three thousand other harmless websites that I often browsed.

As it happened, couchsurfing *was* pretty popular and there were thousands of hosts, eager and willing to offer a stay in return for a few hours of 'practising' English with me.

It was a good start but I knew I would have to overlook most of the places I had set my heart on and go with the flow. There was no reason to treat China differently from all other places that I had explored on a whim and on that optimistic note I sent out couchsurfing requests and three days later found my host.

I liked Deborah Luo the moment I saw her profile picture. She was cuddling a tiger in Thailand. She was also just forty-five minutes away from the airport on the subway. Any destination reachable in under an hour in China was considered 'close by' and I was fine with it. Debbie was an exchange student from Suriname at the South China Agricultural University and although she was of Chinese origin, was more Surinamese than anyone I have met and spoke Chinese as well as English, which was the ultimate deal maker.

Here, I make a slight detour in my narration. I did briefly consider joining a group of travellers or bikers who didn't mind a pillion or a tour group open to suggestions and taking risks. From Googling the soy out of China's travel scenario, reading blogs and travelogues I'd learnt it was not an easy place for travelling, thanks to the language and size and the more I read, the less I liked it, but the pictures were so exciting and quaint that I decided not to give in to prejudices till I had actually travelled there. If the less brave ones had given up on China due to limited patience levels and inability to cope with cultural differences, it was their loss. I would be *The Others* who didn't shrivel in the face of challenge. I wouldn't bypass hardships by heading to Shanghai. I would find a way to climb mountains, eat scorpions, overcome every linguistic impediment and get under the skin of China's smokescreen.

China was going to be the biggest challenge I had faced as a solo traveller but I would take it on happily.

Years ago when circling over Jacksons International Airport in Port Moresby waiting to land, I had been very apprehensive, wishing that I had never left home. Circling over Guangzhou waiting for permission to land was not quite the same thing, but I felt exactly like I did in Port Moresby. A horrible thought popped up in my head.

I am going to die.

Again, when crawling ahead in the long immigration queue in Guangzhou, I had the same thought. *Okay, now I am going to die.*

I have no justifiable reasons for feeling this way. It was just one of those moments when thoughts go south perhaps due to lack of sleep? I would never know.

This unexpected delay put me a little off track. Would Debbie wait? What were my options if she didn't? I would of course return to the airport and sit the night out and that thought depressed me, yes, but not enough to want to die.

Debbie's instructions had been clear.

Get on the Metro Line 3, interchange at Tiyuxilu to the other part of Line 3 that heads towards Tianhe Coach Terminal. Your stop is Wushan. Take Exit B.

I arrived at the subway only to see that China's metro system was not as simple as Debbie made it out to be. Firstly, it was full of people, and secondly, Tiyuxilu was pronounced very differently from the way it was written. Thirdly, of all the people I spoke to, no one seemed to know of Tiyuxilu or didn't want to help me. It took me twenty minutes and four missed trains to figure out Metro Line 3.

When I finally boarded the train, the thought returned. *I am going to die.* To be fair, when that happened, I considered it a welcome option.

The flight had been long and I was not exactly a barrel of laughs. The simple task of locating the metro station had not been so simple and being the only foreigner and perhaps the only

English-speaking person on that long ride in a packed train made me the subject of frequent and curious stares.

Then something happened that snapped me out of these depressing thoughts.

On the subway was a young boy with a concave stomach and a fondness for practising English on foreigners. Since I was the only foreigner on that train, he seated himself beside me and started talking.

'Where are you from?'

'Dubai.'

'Dubai? Yes. Dubai. Very good country. I welcome you to China.' Here he bowed a little.

'Thank you. You are kind.'

'My English name is Joseph and my Chinese name is Xiao Zhang.'

'Well, hello, errr…Joseph. Glad to meet you.'

'Thank you very much, miss. May I help you?'

I saw here a golden opportunity.

'Can I use your phone please? Or wait, perhaps you could speak to my friend and tell her where we are right now and how much time it would take for me to arrive at—uh, Wushan?'

I should have used shorter sentences and for that lapse I had to repeat myself thrice before Joseph whipped out his phone and called Debbie.

Debbie was going to wait for me. Bless her.

'Thank you, Joseph. That was kind of you.'

'You are very welcome, miss. I learn English at University. I want to practise English now.'

So for the next twenty minutes, he talked. Joseph, in a cute, bookish way, asked me what I did, where I lived, if I was married, how long I was going to stay in China, about India, about Burj Khalifa, before going on to tell me his age, name of his university and his girlfriend's name.

But around the time I was mumbling about Burj Khalifa, my attention was diverted by some pretty young girls with extremely short shorts, lacy tops, oddly shaped hair bows, no-maintenance-needed-skin, and mobile phones from which hung a variety of animals. I watched them as they giggled in that strange Chinese way. I couldn't help but look down towards their legs that ended at the heavily decorated platform shoes and wondered why all the wax came from China when their women never needed waxing.

A particularly exotic specimen came to stand by my knees and I followed her extremely silky smooth legs to her panty line as Joseph continued practising his English. I watched her muscles tighten as she spread her legs apart to balance herself with the train's rhythm but did not look up from her mobile phone into which she typed with alarming speed. She had a fantastic balance and why not! Surely she must belong to the clan that gave the world martial arts. Who is to say that some of that envious talent was not coded into her DNA? Perhaps she could even do the *Crouching Tiger Hidden Dragon*?

These thoughts were broken when the train jerked. The exotic creature suddenly threw up her arms and grabbed the handrail.

Since I was looking at her anyway, I saw something that made me inhale sharply. My eyes had come to rest on a small but determined bush straining to get out of her armpit.

I looked away. It was not just that exotic creature. It was almost every other girl within my periphery on that subway that morning. China definitely needed to rethink their wax exports.

Debbie was the kind of host you expected to couch with if you ever considered a life of travel with free stays. She was the bubbliest girl I had ever met since arriving on Chinese soil and often I felt I was meeting a version of myself.

She suggested dinner right away.

'Let's get you some real Chinese food, you must be hungry.'

Thank God, Debbie was Surinamese-Chinese but spoke like an American.

'Do you eat pork? I know a restaurant where they have some real good stuff. Unless you are keen on eating something else? Dumplings? Or say, noodles?'

'Your suggestion—I am game for anything. And yeah, I eat everything that has once lived.'

My body needed food to adjust to the new time. I was eager to taste Chinese food in China and it was important to get the first meal right. Or else, my impression of China would forever be tainted.

Debbie's knowledge of local cuisine differed from what I had heard from people who had visited China. My own experiences with Chinese food had been limited to Indo-Chinese dishes such as fried rice, chicken dishes and soups named after various Chinese provinces and made by Chinese-looking people from North East India. But I had liked it.

Debbie, who loved food, didn't see it my way.

'What's Schezhwan fried rice?' she asked me as though I had just made that up and pushed a menu towards me. 'Never heard that one before.'

I was inclined to agree with her.

'You know how it is with us Indians. We are so great at rebranding. Come on, let's try something exotic then—say, dragonflies on a stick?'

'Oh, for God's sake, there are not enough dragonflies to feed the entire nation, trust me. We occasionally eat other stuff as well.'

We laughed at this. I hadn't had many enriching conversations about Chinese cuisine because every person I knew who had been in China had started and ended with weird, exotic and domestic animals and while that wasn't really off-putting, rearranging my belief in pseudo-Chinese cuisine was the difficult bit.

My first real meal changed the way I perceived Chinese cuisine. To say it was a disaster would be just about right. So let me begin with the way it arrived without a fork or a spoon, which was the real tragedy.

Like Mandarin, the Chinese ritual of using two sticks to shovel food into the mouth has long tested the patience and skill of many a traveller. You eventually learn to balance large meat balls between two thin sticks held in one hand, but when you are hungry it really is…very annoying.

Debbie came to my rescue. But she made an observation first.

'You have travelled so much—you should have learnt how to do this,' and launched into a practical demonstration on the use of chopsticks, pushing my middle finger under one and placing my thumb over the other before showing me how to move my index finger rhythmically with the thumb to sort of form a long tweezer.

I am not a quick learner. I tried and gave up when I dropped the egg drop for the third time.

I had a finger cramp from trying too hard and watched in slight annoyance as Debbie expertly held up vegetables, noodles and meatballs between her sticks.

'Move your fingers up,' she instructed between mouthfuls of noodles. 'That should make it easier.'

Easy indeed. I was still having an enormous amount of trouble.

'I swear eating should not be that hard. Of all the things invented to eat rice, how did chopsticks get an edge in?'

I cheated by asking for a fork. Yes, I was that uninspired foreigner unable to use a set of chopsticks in a forkless restaurant.

'Really, why would anyone use a 1200 BC technique to eat? I mean look at you guys, so advanced in everything else, but this? Gosh, why can't I just get a fork or a spoon?'

'Because this is China, Anjaly. For God's sake, try.'

Various thoughts kept running through my mind as I stared at the chopsticks and my untouched food getting cold.

'I have no idea what is going on, Debbie. How about I stab the food instead, like a, err, kebab? Or hey, wait, what if I scooped out the vegetables; after all, I have two sticks and if I placed them together, I have a, sort of scooping device? It worked with a branch when camping outdoors, so why not now? If I am going to eat one strand of noodle at a time, how long would it take to finish this bowl?'

I didn't stop there. 'Okay, I feel like a total loser. Moron. But I am going to use my hands instead. Indian style.'

In the end I just jabbed at the meatballs and ate them as though eating them off a skewer. I don't think Debbie liked me much after that. I also learnt later that it was rude to leave your chopsticks sticking up in a bowl of rice.

It was lovely walking through the atmospheric and beautiful lush green university campus. It also seemed strangely out of place. Debbie's apartment was lightly furnished, simple yet quaint, a typical student's pad. I liked it there. We stayed up late talking and I hoped the jet lag wouldn't bother me much on my ride on the world's fastest train the following morning.

My last question to Debbie before we called it a day was about the Chinese women who left their underarms unshaven.

Debbie laughed. 'Wait till you get to Beijing,' was all she said.

I didn't like the sound of that.

The next morning I was on a train committed to its reputation as the world's fastest long distance train doing 300 kmph and unlike what I'd originally thought, my seat did not rattle, shake or shiver, the countryside was not blurred and the water in the bottle on my window sill remained still.

I was as elated as anyone travelling on a super-fast bullet train in China for the very first time would be.

Under the circumstances, writing was a breeze.

Dear Diary,

I am on THE TRAIN. This is absolutely WOW! I don't see many people on the train excited to be on it, with the exception of me, but pretty much since my arrival, I haven't seen any emotional outbursts from the denizens over anything—feels a bit robotic—but then I am Indian—we are so full of drama.

This girl beside me and the one next to her have fed me micro-chicken parts from vacuum-sealed bags, dehydrated fruits and caramel popcorns. And it is amazing how everyone on board is carrying food. There can be no shortage on this train for sure…that starched blue-uniformed female attendant comes by every half an hour with a food trolley which is great, but the smell of noodles and soups is getting a bit too overpowering.

I like what I see outside my window. Huge expanses of green and I suppose we are experiencing many geographical and climatic variations as we travel at great speed through rains, blue skies, green fields, undulating hills, rivers, patches of barren land. China is indeed very big. I don't suppose I would have ever realised how big had I not taken this train. This train is remarkable. Will I live to see a similar train in India?

What was said about the Chinese technology and their knack of duplicating everything in the world? Surely, this train is not a spin-off on anything else. That is for sure.

I think I will survive China.

Two hours later…

> *That was a nice nap. Didn't realise I was tired. I love the way this train rolls so rhythmically, so great for a nap. There is one little concern though—I tried getting information about my hostel from people on this train, but damn, no one really speaks any English. In half an hour I will arrive in Beijing. I am a little nervous, yes, for I am not entirely sure how to find the hostel. If fatigue doesn't kill me, getting through this language barrier will. That's for sure. Nervous? I am that, all right.*

Beijing station was a maze. It was hot. It was also full of people.

Correction. It was full of people with one or more tablet-sized mobile phones into which they stared or punched numbers while being completely unresponsive to the anxious tourist trying to grab their attention. Okay, so China did have a very large number of people and it was reasonable enough to expect a fraction of them to be somewhere, but when all of them appeared to be lounging about the railway station it said bad things about the reason for their existence, didn't it?

And interestingly every signboard was in Chinese. My thoughts naturally became slightly racist.

Why are the Chinese not like the Thais who start their day with a smile and a purpose that is so tourist-centric? It would be so helpful if they did. I wish there was a way to get them to react.

I walked, pushed and crawled my way through, tapped a thousand shoulders, showed papers with the hostel address, made signs of a metro and gestured requests for the use of their phones. When nothing worked I began to fear I would get lost and remain lost and no one would find me. That thought made me slightly hysterical. What the hell was I going to do?

If I could locate the metro that would take me to Dong Si, I *could* somehow find my hostel if I followed the correct signs to the Hutong Area which housed the Happy Dragon Hostel. But getting out of the ocean of mobile-wielding locals was my primary need.

At this point, you would ask why a seasoned backpacker who excelled in finding the needle in a haystack would worry about things going wrong. Weren't I and everyone who fell in the aforesaid category renowned for our ability to find the said needle?

What could go wrong?

China had the answer to that question. Everything.

I did not come to Beijing to lounge about the railway station and when every one of the thousand heads nodded negatively to my request, I began to doubt the very existence of the metro. The metro sign around the world, if you are attempting to speak in sign language, is the same and I was sure I did that right. It didn't work.

Finally, I spoke.

'Where is the metro station?'

A kind man pointed straight ahead.

Moments like this show up your deep-rooted biases. Why the hell had I been gesturing all this time? Did I think that everyone in China was deaf and mute or understood no English? Come to think of it, I had unconsciously switched to gesturing ever since I got off the train. I really needed to rethink my communication strategy. Was I really that biased against the Chinese? Perhaps, and that was not good.

Thoughtfully, I followed his directions. I was not completely satisfied with just knowing the way to the metro; I needed a fall back plan for the just-in-case situation. As long as I stayed within the vicinity of the train station, there was a slim chance I could get on a train to someplace out of Beijing if it came to that or maybe I could spend the rest of my time on trains, criss-crossing the country at random. Those were attractive possibilities.

Instead, I ended up in the taxi park. China was indeed mysterious.

After a brief thought, I gave in. I hailed a cab and in that serendipitous moment the cabbie rolled down the windows and said, 'Where you go?'

Yeah, that *was* English. Hallelujah.

He then asked if I had a number. 'I call your hotel, you pay five Yuan extra.'

A cut-throat he was all right, but worse things could have happened if I had lingered around.

There are easier ways to get to Downtown Beijing to the hostel, such as hostel pick-up that would set you back by RMB 250, a fair price considering the unhappy encounters you can avoid at the station but it was not an option I had the sense to take. But this was cheaper.

As we crawled through the traffic, I told myself I should have also learnt a bit of Mandarin.

Kàn?

Happy Dragon was an ambitious name for a hostel that had Sally at the reception, who, upon my arrival asked me to pay for the previous night because I had not turned up as promised.

'The bed was empty last night. You pay for yesterday. Eighty Yuan.'

And even before I could react, said I would have to move the next morning as the hostel was full.

Three days before I left Dubai, I had reserved a bed for two nights at Happy Dragon Hostel, but that had been before I had a ticket on the Guangzhou-Beijing bullet train. When I did get a confirmation, I had duly emailed Mr Lee cancelling the first night's stay. I left Dubai without checking for his reply which apparently he hadn't sent.

'You check out tomorrow, okay? No room. All full,' she stressed. 'We book for you at Dragon Courtyard if you like.'

'You mean, in exactly twelve hours from now?'

'Yes. We are fully booked.'

When I insisted I had emailed Mr Lee about the cancellation, Suspicious Sally urged me to 'show' her the mail and, without waiting for me to respond, logged on to the hostel computer.

'Show me.' If she weren't Chinese I would have thought her rude.

So I did.

Small victory. As I advanced to my dorm, she called out—

'His email address has changed. You should have written to that.'

Sure Sally, Mr Lee has every right to change his email address. How about if he'd conveyed that to me as well? Would save everyone some little trouble? God knows it is hard enough to get here—and what do you know, I have to move again tomorrow.

I was hungry. Suspicious Sally suggested walking around the Hutong Area behind the hostel.

'There are too many places to eat here,' she added proudly. 'All tourists like Chinese food, you walk here, find many places,' and directed me towards the night market where she said I could also find cheap clothes, namely underwear, which I was in need of.

She was all right, was little Sally. I wondered what her Chinese name was.

Hutong roughly translated into a neighbourhood of narrow alleys alongside which are doors that open into courtyard residences. Although many of these traditional hutongs are disappearing to make way for new houses, Beijing does have a few left. It was a whole new experience walking through these narrow lanes filled with makeshift shops, vehicles, potholes, dirt and people who repeatedly cleared their throats, spat and screeched.

I found cheap underwear. The seller punched in a number on the calculator and pushed it under my nose.

20 Yuan.

5 Yuan.

She grabbed the calculator and viciously jabbed at it.

15 Yuan.

I went up by one.

We hadn't spoken to each other, preferring to alternatively jab the calculator. It was how bargaining worked here. As the tempo increases the jabs get harder and vicious, but as long as the calculator passes hands, you have a fair chance of closing a deal. You worry when the seller puts away the calculator after looking at your price.

In the end, I paid 7 Yuan for red and black underwear with strategically placed hearts.

Clutching my goods I stumbled around the street hoping my nose would guide me to the food market but with the confusion of aromas I had to rely on my ears to catch the sounds of hissing stoves or eyes to look for steam clouds rising from a cooking pot.

My combined senses took me to the hub of the food market and as I walked along scanning the food on display, all I saw were scorpions and dragonflies of varying sizes mounted on long sticks, piles of dumplings sitting on boiling pots, noodles sprinkled with baby scorpions, slices of stinky tofu that looked like chunks of snake and heads of dogs hanging by some invisible rope at the centre of it all.

In the split second before I vomited, I had the vision of being in culinary hell.

Not that anyone cared. I am sure if I had passed out on the sidewalk, no one would spare me a glance. Vendors would continue to sell while buyers would continue to cough and spit and carry on eating. Yeah, the Chinese were like that.

ꕥ

I wanted to cry but my need to get out of Hell Street was strong and I did not stop to see the horrific scene of little scorpions scrambling away from the plate of noodles someone had ordered.

I spent the night in the hostel bar drinking jasmine tea and writing in a book and occasionally joining the conversation taking place around me. It was hard to explain why I was drinking jasmine tea which was essentially like hot water but cost a lot more and not beer or anything else.

I went to bed hungry but my mind dwelled on our long dead dog thoughtlessly named Tiger, who during his short life had been very faithful. In honour of his memory, I swore I would never eat dog meat again.

ꕥ

Dragon Courtyard sat on a neat little property located in a cleaner neighbourhood. The dorms were bigger, there was a real café with leather seats serving American and Continental breakfast so it goes without saying that coffee was served here too, Western style, and in China that meant a lot to a coffee addict. By that I mean myself.

The following day, I joined a tour group and headed for The Great Wall of China in what was the second highlight of my trip. The Mutianyu Section, we were told, was free of crowds, isolated and involved a longer ride through the countryside, but the best thing about it was our chance to walk on the wall without bumping into fellow travellers.

'You will have you own Wall to walk on,' our expressionless guide told us repeatedly when he thought he was losing our attention. Going by the number of people on the bus, I cut myself roughly eight kilometres of the Wall to walk on.

The girl seated by my side whispered to me.

'He is lying. Nothing in China is without people. They are everywhere.'

'I agree. But Mutianyu is far, so there might be some truth in what he is saying. Yes? Oh, I hope so.'

'Wait till you get there. It is hot and you cannot walk much. But I have been told there is a cable car that would take you right up to the Wall. I am not going to walk in this heat.'

'I am not either…It is hot, isn't it?'

We became friends after that. The Mutianyu Section of The Wall was everything the guide had not told us.

We had arrived straight into a tourist war zone. Tour buses were everywhere. Private vehicles were everywhere. Hawkers were everywhere. We crawled uphill to the cable car booth and queued up. Everyone that morning seemed to be waiting for the cable car.

It was hot.

A thousand other first timers who thought they owned exclusive rights to the eight-kilometre stretch of the Wall agreed on two things:

It was hot.

The Chinese knew how to make walls.

The second was particularly true for no matter how many pictures you have seen of the Great Wall, standing on it shook the basics of your imagination. Everywhere you turned, you saw The Wall. Perhaps from above it would appear as long, fluid arms stretching far into the deep jungles interspersed with tall watch towers and if you could somehow ignore the people crawling all over it, it was indeed a beautiful sight to behold.

This section of the Wall was the example of strength and weakness of the Ming Dynasty (1368–1627) although how they explained the weakness is beyond me. The Wall was an example of sheer strength and to a tiny extent, madness.

I was not particularly up to walking that morning. It was hot but that did not deter the athletic-bodied visitors and the determined ones from climbing towers, running or walking really fast to cover as much as possible in the short allotted time. I was content to look around. I had many questions. I was awed. I was humbled. I was proud. I thought of the stories I could tell my family and friends.

I must have been lost in my thoughts for a while because a tall, young tourist slid up to me, leaned through the opening in the Wall and whispered—

'It's magnificent, breathtaking…beyond the imagination, don't you think? No matter how hard I try, I can't imagine all of it. But hey, it's just a really long and elaborate cemetery ever built.'

'Huh? What? Oh, you are right. I just did not think of it that way.'

It was true. If you thought about it, it really was that. Those giant rocks did not go up the undulating hills by themselves, right? In an era when cranes were non-existent and rulers depended solely on the labour force it is only reasonable to assume a good number of men hauling those stones uphill to have come in the way of misfortune. The young man was right. But if you can separate that harsh truth you can see the sheer genius of a visionary who built a wall long and strong enough to keep Mongolian warriors from encroaching upon their land.

It was a manmade wonder all right, never mind what you called it.

If I ever went up in space and spotted the biggest cemetery in the world, I would know I was orbiting over The Great Wall of China.

The lunch that followed was one of the best meals ever I had in China, the reason being that it was not real Chinese food. It was the kind of food that tricked tourists into thinking otherwise.

Fs OF CHINA

The next day I suffered my second heat attack since Kampala, at the Tiananmen Square soon after getting myself photographed in front of the gigantic picture of Mao separated by fifty metres of manicured lawn and armed guards. I passed out on the sidewalk and only miraculously escaped being run over by the millions of tourists marching around the historical area with cameras flashing.

'Are you all right?' a kindly face was speaking to me and through the haze of dizziness I made out the shape of a woman in a skirt with a bottle of water in her hands, some of which was also running down my face.

I mumbled. She offered me a sip. I sat on the hot sidewalk sipping her water as the sun beat down fiercely. The kind lady held her umbrella over my head and offered me a candy.

'Thank you,' I murmured. 'So sorry for the trouble. This has never happened before. Was I out too long? God, it is hot isn't it? I feel better now, thank you kindly, ma'am.'

She didn't leave. So we sat on the sidewalk and exchanged stories on China. She herself was an Australian teaching English at a school in Dalian and was down at the Capital for the holidays.

Briefly I considered a life of teaching English in China but the heat soon put an end to that thought. Passing out on sidewalks in Tiananmen Square was not really a great start to a career of teaching English in Chinese schools.

What I badly needed was food. Ever since my arrival in Beijing and my encounter with heads of dogs and scorpions, I had unconsciously stopped eating, except fruits and the occasional meal at the hostel or flatbreads from supermarkets. It was hot too, nearly as hot as Dubai in summer. Fruits were not enough to see me through the day and the heat. Dehydration was another area of concern. I drank in moderation so as to avoid using the unclean public toilets. But I would eventually have to break this self-imposed fast and force myself to eat, maybe at KFC or McDonald's—anything as long as it was not sold on the streets.

So I go back to the original thought I had when circling over Guangzhou some days ago. *I am going to die hungry in the fourth largest country in the world with the highest population.*

The kind lady walked me to the metro station and hugged me goodbye. To think I had come to China and experienced the kindness of Australian expats instead.

Dragon Courtyard had free barbeque and beer on Mondays which was a blessing. So I got myself every kind of barbequed meat and eggplant and drank a few litres of cold beer while writing in my diary that soon turned incoherent and became sloppy lines across the page. The only other person in the hostel's café was Alex who had had enough of Beijing and was heading to Shanghai on a slow train that would take twenty-eight hours. And he didn't even have a sleeper.

'I want to try standing that long on Chinese trains,' he said over beer and small talk. 'Should be fun, is what I hear. In any case, I have a backpack I can sit on if I get tired of standing.'

At this we laughed as only two drunken people with optimistic views of Chinese trains could and ate more eggplant while the other inmates of our shared dorm slumbered on in the cool air-conditioned room.

God, it was hot.

The next day, realising that I wasn't going to get far being adventurous in a city like Beijing, I stuck to the touristy tracks that took me to the Summer Palace, The Imperial Palace, the Temple of Confucius and the Lama Temple or the Yonghegong Lamasery, all reachable by the excellent network of subways. I was content knowing Beijing this way, not really caring whether I got under the skin of real China. There was fun in getting lost, but in China that meant certain death. My energy levels were low, I hadn't met many friendly faces and I had not been able to chip through the coat of Beijing's indifference.

But at the end of the day I also concluded that if you really want to get lost forever, ask a Chinese for directions and follow it up with another Chinese just to be sure.

I cannot explain why millions of tourists visit Beijing every year, because I was really happy to leave it and begin my real journey through China.

I had seen enough raised arms on the subway not to be fooled by the pretty faces with silky skin. Debbie had been right.

I give China four thumbs for safety. In terms of danger, you need only worry about death by boredom and not much else. Ignore the bile-inducing food and hairy armpits and China had a lot going for it. I don't mean this sarcastically, really, and if you can deal with the above, you are good for China.

Since I was a victim of the first woe, I wrote a lot. Notebooks were cheap and writing had become my real connection with the English-speaking world, besides the occasional chat with fellow backpackers in the dorm. I had discovered what I will call the Fs of

China—fascination, frustration and fun. Each of the Fs depends on your perspective.

Dear Diary
McDonald's, Beijingxi train station

It is extremely odd that my backpack is getting heavier. All I have purchased are three t-shirts, chopsticks, and a book but that couldn't have added to the weight. Maybe I am exhausted and hence feeling not so energetic. Perhaps. I haven't slept well in the last few days, plus it is hot. And Humid.

I feel weak as well, which I suppose is due to the lack of proper food. I don't seem to be able to bring myself to eat much around here. The memory of that evening in the marketplace with the scorpions is really the cause. People spit too much, even around food. So, so disgusting. I am also trying to stay within my budget of USD 75 a day so eating at fancy restaurants is not an option.

I want to write all this before I forget. I find trains in the capital a little packed for comfort. They are sometimes disturbingly full. Good luck finding an empty train or a place to sit. People are always waiting to get in or get out and don't really care if they are pushing their way around. 'Excuse me' doesn't work as well here as it does in other parts of the world and you need to push your way in or out if you want to get in or out of the subway. I mean, really push never mind that you have a big backpack that might cause considerable hurt to the co-passenger. I also have had to trudge up and down the stairs because sometimes the escalators don't work and the Chinese have dug deep into the earth to lay their metro lines. It is a little like climbing Mt Everest or a good-sized mountain. I am glad I am not wearing any platform shoes or heels but I see the girls so effortlessly walk and run in them!

What is worse is that here they don't really care about the tourists. It's definitely not like that in Thailand or Turkey. Here if you think you should get special treatment for being a tourist, you can think again.

Oh, I must stop. Here comes a girl. And she is smiling.

That girl was An Shuanghong.

Hers was the kind of infectious smile that was always followed by a conversation.

'Hello. I am An Shuanghong,' she said like a robot with a lot of practice saying just that. But that had been the case with pretty much every conversation I have had with every Chinese trying to speak English.

An Shuanghong then sat herself facing me over the counter and leaned over dangerously close to my lips. The counter was narrow and I happened to be leaning towards her as well so I almost touched her pink lips and transparent skin. She was fragile.

I pulled back just a little, enough to observe but not touch.

She placed a magazine with pictures of girls in Chanel on the counter and choosing the prettiest of them all, pointed at me.

I wasn't beautiful, flawless, made up or well-dressed, but I am guessing she was trying to tell me that I was pretty.

When a Chinese angel with pink lips, translucent skin, eyes like limpid pools, hair so soft and silky black tells you that you are pretty, you take it as a compliment and have the grace to blush a little.

I didn't do either.

'No way, for God's sake, these women are gorgeous.'

That was too much for the gorgeous angel. Her limpid eyes turned smoky and confused. She pulled out what could pass off for a very big mobile phone and rapidly typed into it.

What I saw as the English translation made me faint—

'In doing? How you doing? The moment you rest!'

For two hours we sat across each other, communicating through her weird translator, some with shocking results and yet understanding each other perfectly.

Who said you needed to know English or Chinese to have a conversation? All you needed was a translator and never mind that it came up with ridiculous results.

At the end of two hours, she showed me a translation that made me teary-eyed.

'Wǒ bìxū líkāi. Zàijiàn.'

Goodbye. I must leave.

And to tide over that awkward moment goodbyes always brought, I turned my attention to her pink handbag decorated with skulls and said—'Very pretty.'

Let me make it clear that I do not carry handbags, pink or otherwise. I think they are unnecessary and pretentious. Handbags are weird.

An Shuanghong had a heart of gold. Even as she battled sudden tears, she instantly emptied the contents of the pink skull handbag into a polythene cover and pushed it firmly against my chest.

'Nǐ ná qù ba.'

She drew two hearts on a piece of paper, wrote our names on the hearts and joined it with an arrow and more Chinese translations later wrote in English 'FRIENDS'.

Then she was gone.

An hour later I boarded my fast train to Xi'an.

I still get emails from the lovely An Shuanghong and in every mail she attaches her photo and expresses her desire to meet me again. I suspect her translator has set it to 'miss you' for all given mails from me.

This one did trip me up though. It said:

'My good friend, and now over how? I miss you! Take me to your family ask students well. Really want to see you and me and shadow, have the time to come to China to play in. I love you.'

With the skull bag safely hidden in my backpack, I was ready for Xi'an. As the train approached the station, my impressions of China underwent a change. It must have been An Shuanghong who set off the Chinese Good Luck, because the train I was on was full of Chinese travellers eager to take my photos and feed me legs of chicken from minuscule plastic bags, dehydrated fruits and crackers till I was forced to use the two words I had learnt. *Bu Xie Xie.*

That meant: *No, thanks.*

I could have fallen in love with China given enough time, that I was sure of, seeing that I was already softening my stand towards the otherwise less-friendly denizens of the country.

In Xi'an, it was easy enough to find Hang Tan House. The instructions had been clear and the handwritten note in Chinese was really elaborate. They even had the name of the metro stop and the direction I needed to take once I exited. The people at Dragon Courtyard had got this one right.

That night I uncovered Xi'an's little secret. It was considered China's Snack City. Damn, I should have headed straight to Xi'an instead of gallivanting about on the Great Wall first.

The Chinese knew their stuff—food, gadgets and ability to cater to every person or industry in the world. That however did not explain why they had built thousands of uniquely expressive warriors and horses and chariots out of clay and placed them in underground tunnels to accompany the first emperor of China into the afterlife. I am of course referring to the Terracotta Warriors of Xi'an. Commissioned by Qin Shi Huang, the founder of Qin Dynasty, these warriors guarded the emperor's tomb, which also happens to be the largest mausoleum ever built over 2,200 years ago. The tomb however has not been excavated out of fear of damaging the remains of the emperor.

It was an important archaeological discovery all right, one made a few years before I was born. There are many pits yet to be opened, but what was there, was impressive. The number of tourists flocking to see the Terracotta Warriors has raised Xi'an's standing as an important tourist destination for domestic and international travellers, giving a huge boost to the local industry.

I even got to meet Yang Xinman, the old farmer who discovered the historical treasure forty years ago when casually digging his backyard for drinking water. The government apparently paid him twenty Yuan, bought out his land and gave him a job at the museum.

Xi'an was a city of towers and pagodas. Take the Bell Tower and the Drum Tower, two important landmarks in the city. You couldn't miss them even if you wanted to put a distance between yourself and the next pagoda. There were more on the outskirts of the city as well and a particularly fascinating one named the Big Goose Pagoda. A name like that immediately set my curious heart beating, forcing me to take the big bold step of venturing out on my own in China to look for the said pagoda after drawing a blank with the handful of inmates of Hang Tan House.

What I had forgotten in my haste to get to the pagoda was having the hostel guys write down bus numbers and Chinese instructions on a paper.

And that is how I learnt that at bus stations in China there were elaborate maps and instructions but if you really needed to get anywhere, you had to know how to draw a basic sketch of the place you wanted to visit.

Even then, you could run into a wall. Like me.

It just so happened that there were other interesting pagodas in the neighbourhood, so the man I was conversing with through gestures, set me on a completely different bus route. As I waited for Bus No. 19 to take me to the pagoda upon the first man's suggestion, the second kind man directed me to a different bus heading to a completely different pagoda.

'Big Goose Pagoda,' I repeated myself with growing frustration and pointed at the bad sketch I had the sense to make on my notebook. Come to think of it, it wasn't a bad sketch of a pagoda I had never seen, but pagodas do share a very common structure and it's hard to tell which one was on my mind.

Then I had an idea. I drew what I thought was a goose, except that the said bird was a mere V, typical of an unimaginative child's sketch of a flying bird. Then I threw in a few more Vs to mean a flock of geese in flight.

'Dayan Pagoda,' said the second kind man, slightly more well-informed in the matter of identifying pagodas or birds. 'Dayan Pagoda.'

So Dayan Pagoda it was.

He didn't stop at that. He proceeded to impersonate a really big bird and sticking his podgy arms out of his back, waddled about. Soon we had a small group of people around us with one suggestion—

'Bus No. 501.'

And because there were at least a dozen people with the same opinion, I boarded the said bus and arrived at the pagoda just as the fountains began their show for the day. Taking that as a good sign, I didn't mind very much when locals sneaked pictures of me when pretending to take a picture of the pagoda and the water fountains, but I can let it pass. I may have done the same on various occasions when I thought the locals were doing funny things.

ꕥ

I left Xi'an with a heavy heart and mixed feelings bordering on fondness for this side of China. I had been told Chengdu was another preferred backpacker destination and was right there along the touristic trail for travellers coming down from Beijing going to the south or vice versa. But Chengdu could not be ignored. Because of the pandas.

I had been booked on a normal train to the panda capital and had, for a small sum, managed to get a sleeper as well. So far, so good.

My troubles began the moment I arrived at the train station.

I had a ticket and I had time. Ordinarily that should have been reason enough not to worry. But when I arrived, there was something really big standing between me and the train that would take me away to another province. There was a queue of at least two thousand people waiting to get into the station. It was as though half the population of Xi'an had turned up just to prevent me from leaving on that train. And going by the way people crawled ahead with their baskets, suitcases and livestock hidden in boxes, I was surely going to miss my train. And that was not a good thought. In a flash of heroism, I pushed ahead through the ocean of humanity like it was my right as a foreigner to go straight ahead.

It worked.

The guy with the scanner let me through when he saw me struggling with my backpack, which was just a pretence to be let through. I was a foreigner and they either really didn't care or they had a way of scanning my backpack as I walked through. I didn't wait to find out what and ran through the old and cavernous interiors and through another sea of passengers that were going to share the train with me.

The rest is left to your imagination. But I assure you that I no more fear people, people screeching, grabbing, spitting, fondling, shoving, pushing or stroking when given a chance in a crowd. I have learnt to push my way through this lot and do so with much glee because I know as I push through my backpack causes considerable damage to anyone refusing to move away. I have learnt to barge unmindful of who gets hurt in the process. China has taught me a lot.

Eventually I made it to the train and found my coach which looked exactly like the t-shirt I had been wearing. The coach, like my t-shirt, had red and white stripes.

I was going on a colour-coordinated ride to the middle of China. What fun.

Dear Diary

I am on the train. I made it. That feels like a huge achievement in itself.

The air-conditioning doesn't work. I am hoping that it will eventually come on, but to switch it off and let the passengers simmer and cook in the heat is not a good thing in my opinion. There is a bed with two pillows and a blanket thick enough for the Siberian cold. But why?

I am hungry. Food on Chinese trains is quite uninspiring and I want something that does not look

> *or smell like noodles. Railway platforms here do not have food stalls—like in India. I kind of miss that chaos and the smell of food on the platforms—but what's that? I think I see a man selling something. Flatbread and chicken? Whoa, I wish these windows would open.*

The one welcome distraction on the train was the coach attendant. A rotund fellow with the friendliest face after An Shuanghong, this man also had a great sense of humour and liked Bollywood movies, the dancing, in particular. In the morning, I caught up with him in the pantry and over bad coffee, he showed me a Bollywood step that could have been a cheap Chinese remake.

He shook his head from side to side, threw out his arms, twisted his head in a weird manner, skipped a little and pretended to hold on to the table as if he would a tree and sang 'la la la'.

By this time of course we had attracted a small crowd of coach attendants who smiled despite the absurdity of the situation.

To this day, I laugh when I see that video. It is one of those videos that make China seem tolerable.

At Lazybones, Chengdu, I met Conor Walsh. He had been reading work papers by the pool table when I burst upon the scene.

'Working on a holiday?'

He looked up. 'Yeah, kind of.'

I don't know what the conversation starter was but I am sure the Almighty had a good reason to put Conor in Lazybones and thereafter leading me to the said hostel.

Because it turned out that we were staying in the same mixed dorm and were booked on the same day trip to see the pandas the following day.

Conor was Irish, a teacher in a London school and went by the name Ginger. It defined his wild side while *Conor* gave him an air of seriousness. With Ginger you could not go wrong.

Ginger had been in Chengdu longer than I was, so he knew where to find Starbucks. As soon as I could leave, it was to this coffee shop that I directed myself. The place was full of tourists relaxing in deep leather chairs looking happy with their coffees even with very high mercury levels. Whoever said caffeine is not good on a hot day probably had gone to the wrong coffee shop.

I fell in love with China after my third coffee. Yeah, it's true—a caffeine overdose is just that essential element required to make you fall in love with a coffee-less country forever.

At the end of the panda-sighting day, I had changed my opinion about the real nature of these animals. They were cute all right. Cute and cuddly, although if you wanted to cuddle them you ended up paying about USD 500 for a five-minute cuddle, but on this particular day, heat had tired the pandas and all the money in the world did not guarantee a cuddle.

I was at a point when the allure of China was beginning to wear off. It must have been the heat. I hated to step out of the hostel even for a bit, but that didn't stop me from exploring the bustling Chunxi Road and the popular Wenshu Monastery and showing up in the evening at Tianfu Square for the synchronised water show as Chairman Mao looked on.

Things got worse when I was told I couldn't head up to Jiuzhaigou Nature because the roads were closed, thanks to the recent flood. Ginger was leaving the next day and with him gone, there were less chances of keeping myself entertained in Chengdu.

Ginger had said that Guilin was China's best-kept secret. That was it. I decided to go to Guilin with him.

There was no reason to stay on in Chengdu. My train ticket to Guangzhou was not exactly a ticket for a thrill ride either. If I ever put it to use, I would be stuck on a train for twenty-eight hours on a hard seat in a coach full of people who may have purchased standing tickets as well.

By no stretch of imagination could I see myself loving this ride, so I cancelled my ticket and hoofed it to the airport with Ginger the next morning without a flight ticket to call my own.

The airline tradition of saving ONLY business class tickets for the last put me in a spot.

I could take it or leave it. The Chinese were straight like that.

'Let's have a cup of coffee and think over it,' suggested Ginger and I saw no reason to disagree. It could be the last coffee I was ever going to have with this man, till perhaps the world closed in into a very small tight ball and we were squished together somehow, so to Costa we went.

'So I guess this is it,' I said with forced cheer. 'I will perhaps get a ticket for tomorrow, but I might just change tracks and go instead to Kunming. Whatever comes along first.'

'Yeah, that sounds like a good plan. Kunming should be fun too.'

Half-heartedly I gave the ticket to Guilin another shot. And miraculously, Shandong 4764 found me an economy ticket for USD 100.

Guilin was on.

But something was happening at the check-in counter.

Conor was waving his arms wildly and speaking in his 'teacher voice' trying to get his message across to a Chinese woman who had no clue what he was saying.

'I am sure I did NOT book a first class ticket. Why, this is absolutely shameful. I do not want a first class ticket. Give me an economy ticket and my money back.'

That, however, was not an option, because there was no economy ticket available. I had been given the last one.

I somehow felt responsible for his loss.

Someone else walked up to him.

'Sir, we cannot make refund. No policy like that. You travel first class.'

This started a fresh round of vehement refusal.

'I did not book a first class. There was no such option on the website. There should have been, don't you think? Now, can I please change my ticket?'

I would have been upset too, if I were him. As a traveller, I didn't see any point in paying twice the price for a ticket on a flight that would take one hour to Guilin. Ginger was led away to another counter and the flustered lady walked up to me and said—

'Madam, please, what I do with your husband's luggage? I hold it? Yes?'

'Umm, errrr, yeah. Of course!'

And because that assumption had been made and because Ginger did not get his money back, the airlines kindly let me use the first class facility at the airport and later upgraded me to first class 'to be with my husband'.

Ginger was a sport. He didn't stay down too long and to make up for the price of the ticket, we gorged on food and packed every corner of our bags with chips, peanuts, cookies and what not 'for later'. That's how I arrived in Gulin, a place I had never heard of until the previous evening, on a first class flight none of which would have been possible without Ginger.

I think he was my luckiest find in China. It was An's lucky skull bag doing this.

Ginger and I found Wada Hostel after wandering about a little. Guilin was going to be great. I could feel it in my bones.

SUN ON MY BACK AND AN IRISH BY MY SIDE

Conor and I got separate dorms at Wada Hostel but Rachel-the-bubbly-gal who checked us in found me a bed with Conor in one hour. 'Couples stay together,' she said with a wink. 'No fight, stay together.'

There was no point in clearing her doubts.

Wada Hostel was the kind of hostel that made a tired and grubby backpacker feel at home. They had everything a wanderer with a backpack full of dirty clothes could wish for—that was called the Laundry Room and it was into this room that Ginger disappeared. I did not follow. When it comes to doing laundry, I am not exactly a willing candidate, preferring to buy a t-shirt or two when the old ones get too dirty to wear. I also root for use-and-throw underwear, same goes for socks and even on home ground, I prefer to keep away from the washing machine.

Ginger did not think too highly of me after this, because he had concluded I was a spoilt brat for not doing my laundry. I did try to explain to him the circumstances that lead me to become 'undomesticated' but he was a teacher and thought everyone with the slightest conscience must do his/her own stuff.

But his attitude changed slightly when an hour later we decided to explore the picturesque town of Guilin on foot.

ꙮ

Through the cobblestoned main streets we walked, passing old men with white beards smoking silently, failing at reading Chinese road signs and getting lost in the end. While moving down the narrow street, the traffic continued to flow somewhat fluidly until we came to the Walking Street. Then it was the people. We had to walk sideward at times to avoid getting washed away in the ocean of human bodies that flowed past.

'There is no such thing as a low season in China, it looks like. I wonder why there are so many people here?'

'Guilin is quite a popular spot, you know. It is only reasonable to expect a percentage of that billion to be somewhere.'

'It just kills the fun—you can't walk without running into someone.'

Conor spotted a woman chopping chillies and was instantly fascinated. She was also entertaining and put up a show especially for Conor. 'Kada-donk, kada-donk, kada-donk, kada-donk'—the knife fell with perfect rhythm and within minutes she had chopped up a little spicy mound. The chilli would then be put into bottles and sold as dumpling mix and flavourings.

ꙮ

The cruise up Li River was a very touristy thing to do, but there was no alternative. If you wanted a glimpse of China that was hard to find anywhere else on earth, you had to be on that cruise along with fifty or more cruise boats sneaking up the river, with the same number of smiling tourists with cameras, taking the same pictures en route.

But I want to be really honest here—once you leave Guilin and go up the river, you begin to see why it has the reputation it does. The karst peaks along the river banks are gorgeous despite the heat and humidity—or perhaps because of that. One can never tell.

The Li River is so famous for its picturesque scenery that one picture appears on the back of the 20 Yuan note. To prove its renowned status, at the precise spot along the river our guide Rebecca presented a 20 Yuan note for our verification. You could call the Li River cruise total immersion and stress-reduction therapy. Ginger and I and a few Australian girls from the hostel stood on the open-air deck along with some other tourists and immersed ourselves in the gently moving panoramic views of fantastic karst mountains rising sharply hundreds of feet above the green forests. Heads of water buffaloes emerged from the water to watch as we cruised by. With every curve in the river the scenery got more engaging and despite the mayhem on the deck and later the scramble for lunch, I felt at peace.

A hard thing to come by in China.

The town of Yangshuo was in full swing when we arrived—packed to the hilt with tourists not put off by the bad weather. There was no shortage of vendors in Yangshuo selling all manner of street-side delicacies. I had coffee while Ginger helped himself to an ice cream cone at McDonald's.

That was the last I saw of him—sucking on his ice cream cone as he walked away and got lost in the crowd.

I returned to Guilin on a late bus and joined a bunch of just-arrived girls looking for a night on the streets of Guilin. I was tired but Rachel had made staying at the hostel an impossibility.

When I had returned she stopped me.

'Why did you not go with Conor? Did you guys fight?'

'No. We did not. He is going to Vietnam. I am not.'

'You should have gone with him. He is such a good man. Maybe you should go to the Longji Rice Terraces tomorrow? It will take your mind off him.'

'Remember I come from India and we have plenty of terraces there. It's also too hot and humid and kinda boring to go on my own. Is anyone going up there tomorrow anyway from the hostel, I mean? No? Damn. I will give it a miss.'

'No fun without your Conor, eh?'

This was the reason I was eating fat noodles and snails with the girls in the Walking Street (Zhenyang Pedestrian Street) after doing a quick tour of the night market that chiefly sold objects no one would ever find a use for. It was good to be out in the Guilin rain with the streets glistening from the recent rain showers, accompanied by a cold breeze, giggling girls and the confusing smells of Chinese food.

And the next morning, before Rachel turned up at the reception, I returned to Yangshuo on a bus, watching the glorious sun beat down on paddy fields and picturesque villages set within a wall of magnificent karst mountain ranges where traditional China thrived.

I discovered a cave that claimed to have 'Gold Water' and a very healthy way to beat the heat and humidity that gripped Yangshuo at *Mango Mango*, a narrow juice bar specialising in mango-related stuff, which for some reason was represented by two fierce wooden cows.

There was no sign of Ginger anywhere. What was I thinking anyway.

I was looking forward to being reunited with Debbie in Guangzhou after over three weeks of criss-crossing China. On Rachel's recommendation, I took an overnight sleeper bus to Guangzhou which according to her was very comfortable and 'they provided blankets' as well.

I boarded the bus on the assurance that I would arrive on time.

But I must describe the bus, for everything else is irrelevant at this point. This long-distance Chinese bus is oddly built, meaning it is shaped in a way that makes a cattle truck look like a GMC. There is no other place on earth that would ever build a bus capable of reshaping every bone in your body.

There are three rows of bunks that run along the bus, with a top and a bottom bunk in each row. Each bunk is roughly the size of a crib or a small coffin if you want another comparison. You can fit in somehow, but once you are in, you stay in. The headrest of the adjacent bunk is raised so that it creates a hollow space around your feet which is where your feet goes—and stays. You cannot turn in the bed or sit up. You can only lie there with your head elevated at an odd angle and wish for the ordeal to end.

A guy behind me however defied the death-row design and sat in his bed burping. I don't know how or why, but what I did want to know was how the hell had he managed to sit up?

I had developed a certain fondness for the Chinese, yes. But that fondness was threatening to wear off inside the bus. Being crammed into a bus with thirty or more of them is not pleasant. Every one of the thirty passengers snort, fart, burp, cough or sniff alternatively or all at once and inside a poorly air-conditioned bus it tends to get stuffy, if not smelly.

It was a good thing that I was only going to be on this bus for about eleven hours.

The bus had a small toilet, about the size of a washing machine. To use this facility you needed to be an expert at crouching, twisting and aiming, which most were not, which resulted in the rather foul smell that quickly spread through the bus because the doors did not lock.

Sometime during the night I dozed off, but when morning came by, I was still alive. And we were in Guangzhou.

Sometime in the night my legs had lost all sensation and it took me considerable effort to pull them out of the bunk and shake them a million times before I could balance myself on them. I stumbled out of the bus and into the sunlight and fresh air hoping I wouldn't pass out of sheer joy at being released from the cattle truck.

I have a feeling that years from now when I talk of travel horror stories, I will be narrating this one.

Hopefully I will be smiling when I say it.

Years ago I had nursed soft feelings for a chap who incidentally had visited Guangzhou and told me fascinating stories about it. During that visit, he had photographed himself under the statue of four rams, a picture I remember because it had sat on my table in a frame for a while before I decided I was over the idea of seeing him in a frame. But I remembered the rams.

To this place I set out with Debbie and, in the process, saw Guangzhou in a way I wouldn't have had I been on my own. Debbie knew it all—underground shopping places, markets, food joints, toilets and the metro stations.

It was in one of the underground shopping places here that we found a food court that looked straight out of an old horror movie. The food was greasy and bad, a blot on Chinese cuisine. But this was also a real glimpse of working China. Workers huddled in small shops underground in the dark. I guess there is a China built underground that one doesn't see so often, but it exists. And it is not pretty.

PEEKING THROUGH THE BAMBOO CURTAIN

Dear Diary

May it be noted that I made the rounds of the rather unfortunate duty free shopping area at Guangzhou Airport as I waited for my flight, looking for a panda I could bring back for my little niece. There were only two stores open and it was only 11 pm. Really, who closes shop at 11pm at an airport? Joanna, my niece, will have to live without a Chinese Panda and I hope she doesn't know that I could have bought one from the centre I visited, but forgot to.

Patience and flexibility are essential and I want to make sense of everything that has happened, so I am going to write about things that really stood out or shook me up, instead of fretting about the lack of a coffee shop to while away my time.

As I write this I am acutely aware of two very alarming words. Culture Shock. Some days it drove me up the wall and right to the brink of sanity and some days it moved me to tears with its extremities, but then it always alternated between two ends of the scale. There was no middle ground here.

My itinerary for China was rather simple. Travel by luxurious high-speed train from the south of the country to the Capital, wander about Beijing and see its famous landmarks as a tourist, travel on luxurious long-distance bus, hike up scenic mountains, eat Chinese food, and shop.

Instead I got a lot more than I bargained for.

In the beginning it was enchanting, but that could be because of all the Jackie Chan and Crouching Tiger Hidden Dragon *movies. However, pretty quickly it began to bother me. Wait, it was a very powerful influence and wonderful at times and charming and I cannot ignore that, but I often felt the Chinese lacked in hospitality and inquisitiveness.*

Why did the Chinese lack the curiosity so common to other South East Asian countries? Okay, perhaps that could be the one reason that made them seem so different from the rest of the world and perhaps that's why, when I think back, it feels like my experiences here were unique. Meaningful? I cannot say that with honesty.

Of course, like the changing landscape, my opinions went through highs and lows and even changed dramatically going from extreme frustration to intense satisfaction although that satisfaction came from seeing the sea of green along the train ride. That said, there was one opinion which was a definitive constant—travelling in China was like an education and every day was like new lessons.

Here I faced some of the toughest travel-related challenges ever—from collapsing due to heat and almost landing up at a different place than where I intended to go, to feeling completely lost and depressed, ignored and misinformed. But I will give China this—it made me a confident traveller. I got to know places that I didn't know existed, Guilin being one such case. I experienced all forms of emotions travelling via the local transportation (I love metros, trains and buses), and was thrown into the deep end without guidance, time scales and restrictions and yet survived.

China definitely is not a solo-traveller destination and I thought singletons like me stood out like a sore thumb amongst the travel groups, expat teachers and couples. It is a land of frustration, fascination and some fun—it does have a lot to offer. I did occasionally seek comfort in the modern amenities and McDonald's but in equal measure, once I left Beijing, I did give street food a good try.

In the end I realised that despite being a linguistically challenged backpacker, I did have fun travelling on fast trains, slow trains, local buses, metros and ferry rides, being the listening post for locals wanting to practise English, eating bao zi, *a kind of dumpling, for breakfast, lunch and dinner, bargaining for fruits, being amazed at the 'live markets' and finding mango juice in Yangshou. No way am I going to get this amazing kaleidoscope called China out of my system.*

I didn't fully understand the Chinese way of life, but understood enough to know and respect what they consider sacred. I might need a big dose of Africa to get over China, but that is not saying that I don't want to come back. I do. I can never ever read a map in Chinese or find a menu that is in English or one that has pictures in it, or find a clean toilet, but I will come back all the same.

What really surprised me is that most of the Chinese don't speak English. Even the receptionists in the hotels barely scraped through, often lacking the knowledge of the language that most of their guests spoke. It shouldn't be so, I thought. Beijing is a big city with millions of tourists and expats and one would assume some of that would have rubbed off on the local populace. But again, I suppose it's wrong of me to want that, merely because the language impediment that some of us faced was so severe. The true fun of being in China and feeling it was the huge language barrier. I am sure there are those who speak English, but I wasn't lucky enough to meet any.

After three weeks of being without a constant friend or a tour guide, I was finally able to understand a bit of the country that was so vastly huge. Also adapt to the culture a little. I was able to order my food and buy some food stuff. I can understand (a little bit) what others are saying.

Way to go, Anjaly.

It is impossible to see it all in one trip unless you are planning to spend a few months going from one corner to the other, and like I did, you might love it or hate it or come back with neutral feelings, but as I write this I think I am falling in love with this country. I think I have also talked myself into coming here again and doing the things I didn't on this trip.

Randomly formed group travel allowed me to see places that would have been extremely difficult to get to solo, or which were not offered as day trips or short excursions from my hostel. Sure, there would have been a way, but not without losing precious time and sanity perhaps, plus the risk of not having anyone to talk to would have been the final nail.

If you intend to backpack and stoically refuse to learn anything about the country before you travel in it, well, let me spoil it for you by jotting down my thoughts here.

It always helps to carry the name of the destination, train stations, location of your hostel in Chinese and try not to mix it up with the other notes you may have. I say this from experience—having mixed up the papers, I showed around the one that directed me to the train station in Chengdu when I was in Guilin looking for the bus to Yangshou. I have also met someone who on the path to Henan had first ended up in Hunan because he could not say it right and hadn't thought of bringing a note from his hostel…and oh, I had almost ended up at the wrong pagoda in Xi'an too…you get my drift?

If you know where you are going and how to get there, well, keep going. A lot of places in China sound similar to an unaccustomed ear and I can bring up at least three provinces you might end up in with a small mistake.

Taxis in general have been a constant source of disappointment. They never stop, never arrive on time and never go where you want to and there is nothing to change that in China which follows the example of every other taxi-system around the world, especially the big cities. And if they speak your language, your options are limited to paying a lot over the meter, agreeing for a unreasonably high fixed price or actually flashing money to get one to stop.

I love train rides, especially the long train rides. In China, it is a very convenient way of travelling, seeing that two cities will always be at least ten to twelve hours apart. But it is an extremely sensible idea to book a ticket in advance. Your hostel can easily book one for you for a certain premium, usually 20 Yuan, because in the absence of a centralised booking system or a booking system in English, this is the only way to ensure you get on a train you intend to board.

ℵℑ

I am going to be a little pedantic about Chinese food for many reasons. One, I intensely dislike people who at the mention of Chinese food say 'bugs'. Or dogs. Some of the common conclusions on the subject I have heard include 'noodles, snakes, dumplings and soup'.

I don't like it at all.

I agree that if a menu is not written in English nor carries a picture of the food, it could be hard to know what you are ordering, but what are the chances that you will pick something off the menu and it would be a domestic animal? That is a possibility, yes, but come on, in a huge country that is China, people grow vegetables, lentils, maize, rice and have poultry and pig farms that produce enough meat without having to resort to only cats and dogs. See?

Don't complain about menus with pictures either—you can easily identify your vegetables, can't you? How about street food? You can see what you are buying, right? And taste and smell?

And who are we to pass judgement on Chinese food? With over three billion people and being the fourth largest country in the world, it would take a lifetime to order all the different dishes China has to offer. Each province has its own speciality and it is wrong to claim that Chinese cuisine is only about cats and dogs when you've hardly discovered their food. The variety of food available here is huge and it could easily take a lifetime to eat through all of them. Spicy, sweet, buttery, cold, hot, crunchy, deep-fried, nutty, oily, peppery, rich, sour, toasted—you've got it all.

Food is a massive part of their lives and the Chinese will pretty much consume anything that has once lived. If you are judging the food by what your hostel or hotel offers you, think again. Pizza, burger and fries, however Chinese-looking, are not real Chinese food.

I eventually learned to eat with chopsticks. I also learnt when to use say Yuan, RNB or kuai. And a few sentences in Chinese that would put an end to a conversation, buy me a dumpling and allow me leave with a thank you, those words being *bu,* bao zi and *Xie Xie.*

I can say *Thank You* in thirteen different languages.

Safak Deniz, my dorm-mate in Turkey may have played an important role in this decision, although she was blissfully unaware of this particular turnaround. She taught me an important lesson that cold December in Turkey. And somehow I couldn't think of Africa without thinking of Safak Deniz.

What was the connection?

So, between returning from China and going to Kenya three months later, I decided to redefine my travel—you know, give it a new meaning. I cannot explain why China felt like an incomplete journey and I admit that as I had sped along on bullet trains through the length of the country my mind had wandered to the dusty plains of Africa. I swear I thought of Africa several times when in DPRK. I had seen the real face of several other countries I'd visited on and off and much of it was far from pretty. I agree there was something far more tangible than the obvious beauty of the places I have been to—an element which helped establish harmony with nature and cement my connection with the place.

When planning Kenya, I began to think of what I really wanted out of the place. Did I really just want to pack a bag and go to Africa because I wanted a break? Could I not do something beyond just satisfying my hunger for the open skies?

My trips into the African continent have been eye-openers. I have returned more knowledgeable about the flora and fauna or *bongo flava*. Perhaps seen a little more of the slums and poverty. I had travelled for photos of lions and Masai warriors as a sort of memory hinge or memory reflector—but I was over that now. I wanted to do something else.

I had, in the meantime, become a travel writer, author, and had a book with Lonely Planet and if you looked me up on Google, I came up in several pages, did guest shows on radio and TV.

But I knew I was missing something essential. I had to find it because I owed it to the world and to myself.

And just as suddenly, Travel & Relief was born. And with that, from being just a backpacker, I became a relief traveller. It was something I should have thought about years ago, but I suppose subsequent experiences on the road culminated into this one moment when thoughts crystallised into one easy and practical solution. Travel & Relief.

I could be a relief traveller as long as I travelled. It was easy and simple. All I had to do now was to get my thoughts in line with my actions. My travelling away from the touristic tracks had given me a wider perspective of the place and its economic conditions and an understanding of the people for whom life's basic necessities were a luxury.

My specific focus in this context is Africa and South East Asia but really, the destination shouldn't limit the scope of relief travel. There were people in need everywhere and adding this to my travel agenda has helped me enjoy travelling a great deal more.

What I had set out to do as part of Travel & Relief was simple. I decided to utilise my otherwise never-used check-in baggage allowance to take along whatever I could that people in the destination country would find useful. It cost me nothing extra to transport goods.

I did find a lot of stuff in my own cupboards, realising that if there was something I had not looked at for the last six months, I was probably not going to use it ever. Six months is a darned long time to leave clothes, soaps or toothpaste unused. I realised that I had too many 'unwanted extras' right there in my cupboard that someone else would find useful.

What didn't fill up my forty-kilo baggage allowance was filled up by friends and colleagues who chipped in with money, medicines, milk powder, soaps, toothpaste, soup, stationery, school bags...and by the end of it, I had more things than I could possibly take!

It was good to see people's enthusiasm for this. It moved me in strange ways and I knew I was on the right path. People signed up to be 'relief travellers' for me in various countries and suddenly I found myself sorting and packing stuff to be handed over to these enthusiastic volunteers eager to be a part of this drive.

I agree that the term *Relief Traveller* does not sound as fancy as volunteer traveller but it is definitely in the same league and independent of any organisation or setup. It is all about adding a little thought to the fun of travel, especially if you happen to be travelling to less-developed countries whose local population is in need of basic necessities. It is about using your skill and good fortune for something new, to be the change through a gesture as simple and easy as carrying an additional piece of clothing or a box of medicines in your travel baggage to be given away to someone in the destination country.

I hope someday this will catch on.

When I finally left for Kenya on my holiday-with-a-mission, I'd managed to send relief material to three countries.

LION HEAD, COWS AND MASAI BRIDE

All of us have at one time or the other flown cheap airlines, unconcerned about long flying hours, layovers or multiple transfers, but I belong to the category which strictly believes that multiple transfers and long layovers are essential to set the mood for a holiday, especially if that holiday doesn't include a plan or agenda. I did have a plan and an agenda but that couldn't have made me see sense in why I wanted a ticket on RwandAir. Perhaps it is my fondness for seeing different airports and browsing through the duty-free stores and complaining about the lack of facilities and good coffee like a seasoned airport critic that does it.

Hence I booked on RwandAir to Nairobi from Dubai. RwandAir didn't fly in a straight line. It first flew into Mombasa, Kenya and then took off to Kigali in Rwanda. Once there passengers were required to board another flight for Kenya thus taking the average flying time from Dubai to Nairobi to ten hours as against four on a straight flight. The only advantage to this roundabout way of doing things was the chance to land at two additional airports, namely Mombasa and Kigali.

I cannot explain why travellers to Nairobi with a short holiday period would take this said flight, but a few did. It made sense if the destination was Mombasa or Kigali, but Nairobi was a different story and I was a part of that story, which is why I bring this up.

We made safe landing at Mombasa, which was slumbering under an overcast sky. A few passengers got off and as we waited for others to board, the inflight music started up.

'Only know you love her when you let her go…And you let her go…' sang Passenger pleasantly through the aircraft speakers and since I had only been recently acquainted with the British singer, I sang along just to show my appreciation.

An hour went by without any sign of new passengers and just about the time we should have taken off, a group of armed men in uniforms boarded the plane and boomed—

'All of you please go back to your original seats and keep your personal belongings with you.'

Then they left. Nothing happened for the next half hour. Then they returned and snapped out another order.

'Bring all your belongings and step out of the plane. Pick out your checked-in baggage and stand by it. Remember you must be absolutely sure it is your baggage.'

While the commotion was taking place inside the aircraft, the rains had descended on Mombasa. We marched out into the tail end of the rains to our baggage wet from the shower and stood by it, waiting for someone to come along and give a thumbs up. The said armed men continued to get in and out of the cargo hold, bearing suitcases and bags and dumping them on the ground. None looked happy.

We had no idea what was going on but the sight of tall, dark men in uniforms do not set the mood for small talk. That done, metal or bomb detectors did the rounds, going over every piece of baggage. I think here I half expected a beep and an eventual explosion but nothing happened. Two hours later we were off again to Kigali. When I looked out of the window I saw four suitcases sitting forlornly on the ground. They had not made it back on the flight.

At this point no one had thought it necessary to tell us what happened and because I couldn't contain myself any longer, I hailed the stewardess and popped my question.

'Three people meant to go to Nairobi got off at Mombasa. Hence the confusion.'

'I am going to miss my connecting flight for sure. What about that?'

She shook her head in sympathy and said nothing. The captain apologised for the delay and assured us of absolute safety. I had a vague idea who the three might have been. One was definitely the girl next to me. I remember how she had been the last to arrive in Dubai and how after landing in Mombasa, had a quick consultation with two young boys after which she had grabbed her bag and shot off the plane.

One thing was certain though—my connecting flight from Kigali would leave without me.

We had four hours to kill at Kigali before our next flight to Nairobi in an airport that was not equipped to provide entertainment or shopping. Kigali Airport was essentially one large hall divided into a coffee shop named Bourbon, a toilet with windows that didn't shut so that anyone who disliked immigration queues could leave that way, and a tiny corner for souvenirs such as Rwandan tea/coffee, a dozen locally made accessories and shawls. In the centre of that hall were scanners and when you passed through that, you reached the fourth corner with a few chairs near the boarding point.

'Must have been a darned empty flight, that one,' I said to a family of four with matching black suitcases. They had the chair next to mine.

'What is this? This is not good,' the head of an Indian family started off without ceremony. 'How can they do like this? We will miss our transport. The hotel was going to send a car for us.'

Indians who miss their flights when on a holiday are not the best people to be around, so with an offhand shrug, I said—

'I am sure they didn't do it on purpose. They probably had a good reason to leave without us—like our flight being extremely delayed, you see? And guess what, it really isn't going to help feeling this way. What say?'

With that I escaped to Bourbon, grabbed a pot of coffee and went to sit by the window to watch the rains.

There's something soothing about the rain. I watched it fall, little droplets pounding rhythms on the airport roof. Being stranded was an absolute blessing. All I had waiting for me at Nairobi was a car to take me to the hostel and there was Peter, the guy who helped with organising the distribution of aid in Kandara and the Masai Mara safari after that. Rearranging my transport was the only bother, which Peter could easily manage.

The airport was charming. The fading brown interior was a preview of the real Africa. But I will say this—if you ever plan a life of travel that includes flying cheap and unreliable airlines, I suggest you carry essentials in your personal baggage, like a hairbrush, toilet paper, toothbrush and paste, a book, or anything that might keep you amused during unexpected and long layovers. The airport toilets in developing countries can run out of paper rather quickly. And always remember that you might never arrive at your destination and there will always be idiots on the flight with you and if you are going to get delayed or deplaned whatever—smile and take a pic. Someday it might bring back memories and laughter!!!

Four hours later we boarded a Bombardier Next Gen airline, which was by far the smallest one I had ever flown on an international route. When the captain announced that we would be flying at an altitude of 34,000 feet, I hailed a crew member and asked where the parachutes were located.

'No parachute,' said the stewardess rudely. 'There are life jackets.'

'Not quite the same thing, are they,' I said without batting an eyelid. 'I was asking about the parachutes.'

She walked away without replying. Yeah, she was rude and just to irk her further I called for coffee thrice and never drank any of it. Don't judge me. I was just being nice in a sarcastic sort of way and there were only so many times I could read the inflight magazine about how cows had enriched lives in Rwanda.

Peter, bless him, was waiting for me when I finally arrived in Nairobi.

ჵ

The next morning I threw my backpack full of children's clothes, medicines and candies into the safari matatu and climbed up in the front for the long drive to Masai Mara, hoping that somewhere along the long road I could distribute candies and clothes to local children. The driver Daniel, an indifferent sort of fellow, only spoke when we fuelled up for the drive where I offered him roasted peanuts and banana. My safari mates, that included Sophie, an American teacher from Doha, her Syrian boyfriend Mahmoud, and a Mexican couple Damian and Clarissa volunteering in Ghana, sat in the back quietly looking out of the window.

Daniel appeared to have no knowledge whatsoever about anything I asked and possibly had the most appalling taste in music that I have come across. He owned one cassette. On one side was a collection of local songs from a bygone era and on the other side, a repeat of the same. And he played them when he didn't want to talk.

We, the safari mates only spoke to each other for the first time at the Great Rift Valley View. After which we had our first breakdown at the base of the valley. Fortunately the place was a long way away from the valley town and we had a long wait, by which time curious children had arrived to 'check us out' and I managed to give away all the clothes and candies.

I was glad to be back in Africa. This was proving to be very satisfactory.

I had quite forgotten what it was like to feel the road under my ass, to have the dust blow in through every window of the creaking matatu, to feel every bone in my body rattle and shake every time the matatu went over crevices in the roads, to have breakdowns in the middle of nowhere, to flag down the next matatu that was no better than the one I had arrived in, the 'long' and 'short calls' undertaken at the bush toilets, to get stung by plants and insects I had never seen or heard of, to shout out Jambo to anyone who cared to listen, to wave at little kids hustling their bony-ribbed herd into the bush as we drove past, to panic when a stray goat made straight for the vehicle at full speed—all this was what I really loved and missed.

It was a different experience compared to riding in Chinese bullet trains, the kind of experience that I thought back of with much fondness. It was true that China did have fantastically cutting-edge technology and infrastructure to be proud of, but Africa with all its rawness was familiar.

Like home.

I think this is the reason I travel—to feel a connection, to understand, to live in the moment that makes life so much more meaningful.

I liked the Rhino Tented Camp even more so because I got a large room instead of the tent I had asked for. Daniel had given us fifteen minutes to check in and regroup at the dining area for our evening game drive to pursue an unlikely goal of spotting the King of Masai Mara in the gathering darkness.

We did eventually spot the Queen lying herself down to rest for the night instead. She didn't care if we had come from far away, were tired or anxious to see her hunt. She just lay down, yawned and closed her eyes.

The sight inspired me to sing. Surprisingly Sophie joined in.

'*...in the jungle, the mighty jungle, the lions sleep tonight...*'

It was wrong on two counts but it fit the occasion. The lioness didn't care.

With the morning tea came the news that 'many many lions had been seen', and that catapulted all of us into action. Breakfast uneaten, we set out to keep our appointment with the King.

'I smell lions,' the news bearer had said. 'I smell many lions. Today you see lions, sure.'

'How can you smell lions?' Mahmoud had asked. He always asked questions but never waited for an answer. He was a little smug like that.

'Interesting how you can smell the lions,' I had offered to the news bearer named Julius. 'What do they smell like anyway?'

Julius wore two thin red-and-white printed, cotton sheets called *kangas*, one knotted around his shoulders and the other around his waist. His feet were shod in black rubber sandals, formerly car tyres. I may have thought my questions would break the tension Mahmoud had created, but Julius didn't really care much about Mahmoud. He spoke to me—

'I dream of lions.'

I suppose if you live by the Masai Mara and sort of socialise with the big cats on a day-to-day basis, there are fair chances of dreaming about them if not actually sleeping with them eventually.

Masai Mara supports possibly the most prolific concentration of wildlife on the planet, so it was a matter of time before Julius would begin dreaming of other species as well.

But Daniel was excited. 'They are Masai, they know,' he explained. 'Even lions are afraid of them, but dreaming of lion is lucky. Today you will see big cat.'

How could one argue with logic like that? Sophie and I exchanged a look and got into the matatu now with its roof open. There weren't many safari groups that morning, which was a good thing really, because if we were going to see the big cat that appeared in Julius's dream, the less people crowding him the better.

On this optimistic note we left on the game drive.

'We go close to the lion,' Daniel, now in his elements, assured us. 'You can smell the lion. We go so close.'

We did eventually smell the lions and it was not a nice kind of smell. He shed some light on the nature of smell.

'Lions don't smell good. They smell like shit.'

He would know. He had been tracking them for years. I suppose if I ever found myself stranded in a game park, I would know which way to walk if I wanted to escape the lion.

Masai Mara is a place where you find all the animals and birds from A to Z, literally. Start with the antelope thrown in with the baboons, cheetah, dik-dik, elephant (or eland), fox, giraffe, hyena (or hippo), jackal all the way to the wildebeest and zebra.

You cannot overlook the possibility that Noah had unloaded all the animals from his Ark right here.

Into these thoughts, Mahmoud infused another, slightly unholy thought.

'I wonder what these fat zebras taste like. I hear there is a restaurant in Nairobi which serves bush meat. I wanna try it for sure.'

I agreed. A visit to the famous Carnivore Restaurant was on my agenda too. I fell in with his idea. 'Zebra, dik-dik and even the wildebeest—I wonder if they are all considered bush meat? What about the crocodile?'

I hoped I didn't sound like an 'animal hater', because I really love animals. But if there is bush meat to be had, I wouldn't shy away; I am a carnivore that way. It was also after this conversation about bush meat, that I learned that Sophie and Mahmoud were going to climb Mt Kilimanjaro after the Kenyan safari.

That evening I returned to the Masai village. A bunch of ramrod straight Masai men walked me around, some of whom spoke English surprisingly well.

I was a welcome visitor and the village headman's son decided to be my personal escort for this evening.

'Come to my home,' he said after collecting an additional USD 5 for this specific visit and led me by my hand into a circular dung-spattered home and I followed him, bent at the waist and manoeuvring ably through a short, curved entrance that abruptly ended at a room in which a cheerful fire was keeping an old vessel of *ugali* porridge bubbling. Ugali is a starchy dish made of maize flour and millet flour and is a staple diet of Kenya, Tanzania and Uganda.

'You eat ugali?'

'Uh uh, no. Thank you. I am not hungry right now.'

That satisfied him. When my eyes adjusted to the dim interiors, I made out a shape lying on a low bench on one side of the fire.

'That is my mother,' he explained. 'She lives with me. I sleep here,' he pointed to another low bench in the dim light but on the other side of the room.

'Ah, nice.'

'And that is for the guest.'

I never really did see what was reserved for the guest because, one, it was too dark and two, he was pointing at the small patch of floor that I was standing on. I moved involuntarily, hoping that I hadn't broken a rule by being in someone else's spot.

He brought out a lion's head and gestured me to follow him out of the hut.

I was glad for the fresh air.

What happened next is one of the most memorable moments of my life.

He placed the lion's head on my head, bowed in front of me and asked me to be his wife.

'I give you six cows,' said he.

By such time a small crowd of ramrod straight men in colourful kangas had gathered around us. Despite their apparent aloofness, the Masai are as curious about foreigners as we are about them.

I saw no way out.

'Six? Naaah, way too less. How about a dozen?'

He did not reply and proceeded to dress me up in his kanga.

I saw Sophie and Mahmoud in the village and called out, 'Hey, come on, I am getting married.'

In the end all I had to show for my wedding was a photograph as the village headman's wife, a picture I cherish to this day.

'Why did you kill a lion?'

'Lion kill my cattle, so I kill lion.'

It made sense when said like that. I suppose Masais were the only living beings that avenged the lions. But oh, they never killed a lioness. No matter what.

It was hard not to believe him. The size of his machete, the determination on his face and the presence of the lion head, that was crowning my head just then, supported his statement.

Then I danced with him and a dozen other guys. Danced like no one was watching. I didn't reach the skies, I didn't quite go straight up like them, but I danced. It made me feel free. They hummed and growled out the traditional song and I danced some more, unmindful of the flies and dung that made a terrible squishing sound under my shoes.

I left before I was required to complete the Masai marriage ritual by spending a conjugal night in his hut with his mother watching. The only woman I had heard of who had married a Masai man was a Swiss named Corinne Hofmann, who had, after eventually returning to her home country with her daughter, authored a hugely successful book, *The White Masai*, in which she claimed that the woman was beaten regularly as a way of restoring love.

The rejected groom walked me out of the village and shook my hands in farewell.

'You come again,' he said in a sad voice. 'You come see me.'

And then he reached into a bag that he wore around his waist, pulled out an old phone and asked for my phone number.

Backpacking or hitchhiking isn't the norm in Africa yet and hence not entirely safe. Yes, there are plenty of expats living here and so you won't really stand out like a sore thumb but safety could become an issue, although it might be difficult to explain yourself why you are in the middle of nowhere.

There is something to be said about Africa though—you are certain to meet a lot of Johns and Jameses. Why? Because, Africa as a whole is full of missionaries and they will not shy away from launching into impromptu Bible lessons. I do not know the best way to wriggle out of a chance meeting with them, but I think a firm no will help. Or if you have the time, stay put. And oh, Johns and Jameses because most of the locals and even the Masais are baptised at birth and given Biblical names.

My own run-in with one such messiah happened on the way to a mall. I had boarded a bus from KENCOM area, behind Hilton Hotel.

He was on the bus and going to the same place as me. He was also very funny.

'What does John the Baptist and Winnie the Pooh have in common,' asked he after introducing himself. It was his way of breaking the ice. I stared.

'The.'

With that he broke into a deep throaty laughter. That was just the start. He was good although I was finding it hard to understand him clearly because he laughed in between sentences.

I asked him if he would like some coffee.

'Yes, but I do not have any money.'

'I am buying,' I said.

He was a preacher, a good Christian.

'I wanted to drink coffee, see, Jesus brought you for me.'

He also laughed at his own jokes and was easy to get along with.

These incidents always restore my love for Africa. And these do not get mentioned in guide books. So I say with conviction—let your guide book stay at home. Speak to the locals who always know best. The trick to enjoying everything African—my bet is this applies to any place you go—is in embracing the chaos and revelling in the freedom like you have never experienced before. You can talk your way in or out of almost anything. Remember that no never means no, and become friends with the hard-working African mindset that anything can be done, either with enough time or money.

A DIFFERENT AGENDA IN NAIROBI

Two days later, as I sat in a matatu with Peter, waiting for a ride to Thika on the outskirts of Nairobi, my mind wandered. The matatu wouldn't leave until the tiniest space was filled up and no amount of complaining would get it moving. Money was passed back through several hands. It didn't seem to occur to anyone that someone along that process would pocket a shilling or two.

I wondered.

People have different reasons to travel, like I had mine. Never mind the lions or the wildebeest, Kenya was rewarding in every way. It defined my travels and my traveller avatar and more importantly, me as an everyday person.

Africa has always been special. I have travelled through the African continent on several occasions because there is a special connect with the place. How can I not love the deep-throated laughter of the locals? The ugali and beans? The casual attitude to any crisis? The matatus with twenty people and their livestock, the dust, the streets that smell of danger at night? The sense of realism?

I loved Africa and everything it offered.

Yes, Africa is a developing country with its share of issues. Yes, it is not as safe as Dubai or Singapore. Yes, transport is not often reliable. Yes, I have issues with food. Yes, I have my share of trouble with thieves and thugs, but that never turned Africa against me.

I have also seen a side of Africa not many have wanted to see.

Kenya has a high number of HIV patients many of them little children orphaned at an early age. Special needs children, people below the poverty line with no access to drinking water either, people living in slums. True, I cannot change their lives forever, but I have realised that if it was possible to change the life of one person for one day of the year, it was an effort well worth it.

Which is why I was on the matatu heading to Thika, loaded with stuff I had brought from Dubai. For all the local stuff, we would source it from Thika.

I was going to give back something to the country that always welcomed me with open arms.

Peter had identified two orphanages in Kandara. I had never imagined that I would find myself in a grocery store in an obscure village in Kenya on a hot and dusty day, bargaining over the cost of sugar, maize flour and beans. But it was a different kind of pleasure for sure. There was a strange satisfaction in knowing that someone, some child somewhere, would enjoy a healthy meal.

I paused over a tray of eggs. Safak Deniz came to mind. Had she found a job? Was she holding out all right? Had she found a decent coat to ward off the Turkish winter? I wished I could meet her again. I had tried to find her after I had returned, but in vain.

Thank You Lord for Safak Deniz. Without her, this wouldn't have been possible.

Like I mentioned earlier, Safak had sown the seeds of Travel & Relief and right now, if I was in Thika, bargaining over the price of eggs, it was because of her.

Peter and I had then loaded the sacks of beans and maize flour into a matatu and headed to the orphanage.

At the end of the long, hot and extremely satisfying day, we had visited Kandara Children's Home and Don Orione Centre for Special Needs, delivered over hundred kilograms of rice, beans, maize flour, cooking oil, eggs, medicines, schoolbags, milk powder, stationery and basic medical supplies to them. I say satisfying because there is nothing more heartfelt than the thankful smiles of those in need. I realised that sometimes a bandage was a luxury for people living here, mainly because there weren't any pharmacies nearby or transport to reach one, and more importantly, no money to buy it either.

ഌ൫

People often look for a larger cause to participate in or an organisation to deal with—but really, that is not necessary. You can be the propagator of your own cause by being a little thoughtful. The important thing to remember is that if you have helped keep the kitchen fires burning even for a day, you have made a difference. I have gone from working with voluntary projects demanding thousands of dollars in the poorest countries in the world to doing my own thing now and even if I don't get a donor book to sign in, there is a satisfaction in knowing that I have been hands on doing something that made a difference. There are a lot of ways you could be a part of this—all it requires is a thought. At the Don Orione Centre for Special Needs, I also came to realise that when you are amongst thirty children who cannot open chocolate wrappers, their smiles mean more than words can ever say.

Maybe it is not always possible for people to spend time with the less fortunate, maybe you don't think you have the resources, maybe. But maybe NOT. If you can afford to fly to Africa for a holiday and spend thousands of dollars to see the wildlife, then surely it's possible to spare a few shillings that can make a difference in someone's life?

Yes. That is definitely possible.

Two days later when I visited Kibera, the largest slum in Kenya located not very far from the city itself, I thought I had walked into another planet.

The taxi I had hired in Nairobi was far from excited to follow me into the slums and only later I saw why. We parked by the edge of the slum but the driver stopped me firmly.

'You must not go inside. It is very dangerous.'

'I must give these things away,' I said, pulling out the box of medicines. 'How else can I give it to them? Surely, it can't be that bad? Is it so unsafe?'

He laughed dryly. 'Madam, you please do not go inside. Leave everything here. They will come and take it.'

I saw sense in that. However, curiosity got the better of me. I wanted to see for myself what made this place so dangerous or unsafe. I had heard about it, about the people who lived in the slums, of the famous 'flying toilet', the incidence of HIV, the murders and the muggings that went on inside the slum, but reading it was one thing and seeing it was another.

I will freely admit that as I stood watching, the slum stirred to life. Faces popped up at the windows, the houses were built one over the other or so it seemed, and in every window was a face. People stood at the half open doors made of cardboard or tin sheets or pieces of wood nailed together, staring at us. There was a distinct smell of human faeces—that explained the flying toilet. Thick black water flowed in the open sewage…I wanted to turn around and leave.

Suddenly the taxi driver called out, 'We should leave. People are coming. It is not safe. Let's go.'

That moment, I understood what he was trying to say. There was fear in his eyes as he pointed towards a stream of people flowing out of the slum, through the narrow path between the houses. They didn't look at all friendly.

'You must never go inside alone. Big group is better. Too many missionaries come in big group, which is okay. Not alone. No. Let's go.'

He helped me unload the boxes of medicines and food.

And just as the stream of people became a flood, we drove away as fast as we could. When I turned back, a scuffle had started.

'They will kill each other for a bar of soap,' he said sadly. 'It is not good.'

I felt strangely disappointed. I knew how vulnerable I was in Kibera, and that was a fact, but I really would have liked to speak to people living there. But I also understood why the people living in the slums behaved like they did. More than being disappointed at not being able to speak with them, I understood a different side to human nature and how the lack of basic necessities changes the very meaning of human existence.

If you are on a trip to Africa (or any developing country), you are likely NOT to use up all you baggage allowances. Use that space to take something that might be useful to the needy. There is absolutely no need to worry about whom will you give your things to, because there are needy people everywhere. If you think pictures of impoverished kids will look great in your album, think again. Those kids are not there to brighten up your album. Give them something in return. Even a piece of clothing or a bar of soap or over-the-counter tablets are of great help.

ജ്

My concept of relief travel was to support at least a tiny percentage of the community, even in the smallest of ways. Being a relief traveller was not about pledging my yearly salary or endless time. It was easy and effortless to donate essential items, medicines or even giving away whatever little I could afford. Every developing country has problems, and poverty is a big part of that, so if you put a little thought into your travel plans, you can easily help a few deprived souls get their daily meals.

If you like flying light, you could buy things locally for giving away. Developing countries have their fair share of needy people you see everywhere and just about anyone will be glad to have an extra bag of rice or medicines. If every short or long-term traveller thought of this, it would be a big step in filling at least some gap in the lives of so many people in need. The local community will benefit from the dollars you spend as well.

It might not be possible for one individual to put aside a lot of money or time, but if a lot of people put aside small amounts it would add up nicely. Involve friends and family—people always have something they do not want. Put your unwanted items to good use, but I cannot stress enough—put a thought into your actions.

There was one time someone wanted to donate a Play Station to a child in Africa who has never seen electricity. I cannot stress enough that giving is one thing, but giving what people really need is quite another.

Although it may seem like both have a lot in common, there is an underlying difference between relief travel and volunteer travel. Both involve a voluntary action towards a social cause. There is, however, a slight difference. While 'relief travel' is independent of an outside source, volunteer travel is dependent on a particular organisation/agency and is bound by time or money or both. Relief travel is a simple act of giving what you want and to whom you want to and how much you want to. Volunteering involves specific time slots or tasks, which may not be the luxury all travellers can afford. Volunteering also involves working directly with the project/organisation on a hands-on level.

The principles of relief travel are totally thought-driven, it requires very little of your time or money—but yes, it does require a thought and a purpose. Anyone can become a relief traveller.

I dislike the question 'Why do you do it?' very much since I don't really have an answer. Well, I have the long-winded response that I like doing it a lot and only for short periods of time. But I don't really do any one thing, in the way people expect you to answer with a professional title or a job description.

The question 'Why do you do it?' is too presumptuous, since it assumes you do something for work. I am doing it because I like to. It makes sense. And I hope to convert one traveller at a time.

THAT'S WHY. AFRICA

I have spent a reasonable number of days in Africa.

Let me clarify. I have spent a lot of time in different parts of Africa at different times on different visits, doing different things. The things I speak of include climbing, trekking, aimless wandering, hitchhiking, camping, scouring secondhand markets, distributing relief materials in slums, and volunteering at children's homes.

On a lesser note of pride—trawling cheap pubs and failing at African hip hop, but then as a traveller one is expected to do this, right?

When I sit down to ponder over why Africa is my first love as a traveller, I realise that the word *different* is the clincher. Africa has always humoured me, accepted me, embraced me, and treated me with a kind of indifference that fuels my inherent desire to conquer it.

If travelling through Africa is on your wish list I hope my reasons will speed up that process. I could go on endlessly but I am aware that the trick to loving this free country full of magic and a lot of third world problems is to start with a mind bereft of expectations. As a travel destination there is no other continent on earth to beat the variation it offers. Its magic works on you in strange ways and once you let it dazzle, you become a captive to its allure forever.

I am under its spell because I opened my heart to it and I am glad I did.

No matter how cultured or well-travelled you are, if you haven't been in Africa, the huge part of your travel map will remain unfulfilled. You might even think of it as a stereotype, as various sources of media are likely to make you believe. I am terribly annoyed when 'non-travellers' feeding off movies, documentaries, development fund campaigns and multiple social media platforms speak cruelly of it or rejoice in the pictures of hungry, naked children on the verge of death.

Yes, poverty and underdevelopment is rampant. Yes, there are no roads everywhere. Yes, there are a lot of little, black, dirty faces—but there is also in-your-face affluence, globalisation and a lot of white faces. People wear expensive brands, buy their 'international' food at supermarkets, goods labelled *Made in China* are easy to find, as are Guinness and Heineken. Yes, people read, preach on roadsides, drag you into religious conversations, cheat and lie—but how is that any different from what you have seen in your home country?

It's not a complete 'lost world' as you may have been lead to believe. It is a real world, with real people. And among these real people and their problems, you find real freedom.

It is the country that brings to life every character from *Lion King*. In its wilderness live Timon, Pumbaa, Simba and Zazu—and they are real. They are the other face of this continent and they are real too.

If you ever suffer from sluggishness, there is cure to be found on the public transport in Africa. I say this with surety because I have travelled on them extensively which, besides helping in the restoration of my faith in the science behind their functioning and the Almighty who ensured safety of the passengers in the absence of shock absorbers and brakes, showed me a warmer and tolerant side of the locals.

To think I would have missed all this had I stuck to the standard touristic tracks! I would never have learnt that back-of-the-truck rides with added exposure to dust could cause unheard of allergies; that snuggling against cattle was not the recommended way to express love; and that smell-induced dysentery did exist.

I would never have heard of the matatu stories born inside its extremely unappealing interiors and on worn-out, sunken seats. A matatu story is as amusing to the listener as it is to the narrator who with every narration unravels the mysterious forces that keep the contraption on the roads. A matatu has seen more than an average local. It moves man, tourists and cattle, accommodates more passengers than Chinese trains and continues to provide satisfactory rides at a very reasonable cost. Its unique identity has been carved out of years of defying God and technology and if you ride in it with your touristic attitude, you are going to feel like a bloody intruder.

Riding in a matatu means sitting with half your ass on the seat and most of you on another person who thinks nothing of pressing his/her body against you and breathing into your ear. It is all part of being the 'friendly African squeeze'. I'd say matatus are ambassadors of patience and adjustments and I recommend riding a matatu as once-in-a-lifetime experience for anyone with the slightest yearning for a real African squeeze.

There have been times I have sat wedged between large women with half an ass on the seat and pushed up against their ample bosoms and on bags of flour with the radio blaring into my ear, but I am yet to find a more exciting way to travel.

Many things about this continent baffled me, but when I stopped finding the reasons for it, I enjoyed it more. It is a huge continent and the variations are wide and unexpected and it would be absolutely wrong to generalise and if you aren't an armour-plated traveller who has never visited a third world country before, you might find it a trifle irritating but that is no reason to judge this beautiful country.

I am no linguist and I am being honest when I say a determined dog could beat me in a language-learning race, but I was fascinated by the fact that when travelling through Africa, you had the best chance of practising multiple languages like French, English, Arabic and what do you know—Dutch. On one of the longer trips, I learnt a little about Swahili and I was content in the knowledge that I knew two of the minor languages that gave it a definition, that being English and Hindi. The primary languages were beyond me—Arabic and Bantu and a good portion of Portuguese.

Africa is one big measure of multiple sensations and, try as you might, you cannot escape the sensory overload nor return without getting desensitised, which, when here could work in your favour.

Time here takes on a very liquid form, flowing slowly and calmly and may be particularly hard at first if you come from one of the time-spinning cities in the world, but assuredly you will get sucked into the casual, devil-may-care attitude towards time, work or anything else that you would ordinarily run after at home. Every time I return to this continent, the first thing I do is forget where I come from and what I do and talk to myself about what I am going to do in the stretchable hours that make up Africa. This also helps me find my mellow side and helps push boundaries of comfort, and a talent to accept the not-so-hygienic practices without throwing a fit appears magically.

You learn to embrace noise, dust and complacency at one go and when all the above seem like things you want to try, you are ready for Africa.

Above all, the allure of Africa lies in its freedom. You walk, you run, you stretch time, you scream, you ponder and you bargain. You complain, you blend in with the locals—you are free to explore.

But you cannot deny that there is a freedom in poverty.

There are some things I miss about Africa in general, starting with laughter. Every person I have met will always greet you with a loud, belly-deep, thigh-slapping laughter, be it at bus stations or villages or a cinema hall. I have never met a happier person than a laughing African.

If you are in the countryside, chances are that you will wake up to crowing roosters announcing the day. Out in the fields are happy children snapping off mouthfuls of sugar cane, giggling as the juices flow down their little black bodies, grinning without a care in the world.

Who says Africa is boring? Try matching the blueness of the skies, the sense of adventure when you begin your ride on the long roads stretching in front of you beneath the crazy blue sky. Africa is big, bold, beautiful and overflowing with adventurous potential. And what about those skyscrapers of Jo'Burg, the mosques of Cairo, Lalibela's churches, Zanzibar's beaches, Kili's snowy summit, the Sahara and the Congo? They are a part of this continent, aren't they? Africa should comprise all of this, so why single out one country and paint the rest of the continent with the same brush and colour?

I miss Africa. I always do. And I will keep going back, even if it is just to distribute candies to children near the airport, dine at Carnivore or buy a book from the evening market on the sidewalk or just to see herds of bony cows walk the roads. I miss Africa. I really do. I miss the price of things. I miss the savannahs and the of animals from *Lion King*. Okay, South East Asia is definitely cheaper but I still miss the rattling matatu rides, the beer and the coffee. It's nice when the coffee is fresh, local produce, but more often than not it's instant Nescafe.

I miss the feeling of the equatorial sun warming my body and making my brown skin darker, I miss the sweat dripping down my body. Most of all I miss the gay and friendly people and their booming voices and their laidback attitude. I miss how they speak and how they sing Justin Timberlake off-key and how they hate it when you bring up Michael Jackson's name. I miss the dust and grime and the humidity in the jungles, I miss the fear of having missed the sight of the mighty lion. Heck I even miss the mosquito nets around the dorm beds, the canvas tents, and the smiling women who served coffee at breakfast.

I miss the coziness of the buses, filled with twice as many passengers as they're supposed to be, and each passenger carrying a bucket of flour, a live animal or an infant child on their lap.

Perhaps I am not thinking straight, but really here it doesn't matter if you are driving on the right or the left—both right and left-hand drive cars are used in both scenarios so it gets very confusing if and when you're on the wrong side of the road.

The buses will always say they are leaving soon, but they aren't. They'll leave the engine idling so you believe they are, and despite high fuel costs, they make the sacrifice as a tactic to try and get the next passengers onboard, which will make their bus fill first, and thus, their bus leave first. If you ask how long a bus takes, seven different people will tell you seven different times, and all of them will be telling you driving hours not including stops, or they'll tell you the distance. Knowing the kilometres unfortunately doesn't tell you anything, because it depends on the road quality, weather, type of car, and whether they have to fill up on fuel or wait for a paid passenger after leaving the bus station.

Hell, I even miss being called muzungu in that familiar sort of way, though strictly speaking I am not one. It is just their way of making you feel welcome.

...SO I TRAVEL

As a means of broadening one's cultural horizons, there's nothing quite like hopping on a train or plane or bus and going away someplace and experiencing something new. But the trouble is, after a while, a weird sort of reasoning sets in and you tend to get a bit worried that you will miss all this when it is over.

Right? Right. So, you travel some more. Because deep in your heart you know it is never really over until you kick the bucket.

But the question is whether, in the midst of all this, you would stop to think about why you travel at all?

Here is something else. Why we travel is not the same as why we should travel, because the first is a completely different question, with its own set of answers that justify it.

The second is, in my opinion, a bucket list waiting to be ticked off, the process of which can be speeded up by travel agents selling package tours who make it out to be a crime not to travel.

And that is not why or how I travel.

So why do I travel at all? I haven't yet worked out the answer to that one, despite the constant debate I have with myself. But I am also not really worried about the answers.

I started off as a hopeless romantic. I thought travelling was going from one place to another and everything was fun and laughter, that it was something grand, something magnificent and a perfect series of adventures. I dreamed of being an eternal wanderer to whom only good things would happen. Now I am not sure if I want only good things to happen to me.

I agree with Paul Theroux who said the wish to travel is characteristically human: the desire to move, to satisfy your curiosity or ease your fears, to change the circumstances of your life, to be a stranger, to make a friend, to experience an exotic landscape, to risk the unknown.

I don't know what makes me want to wake up early in the morning even if I haven't slept all night, what makes me happy in the company of strangers who often do not speak my tongue, I don't know why I don't crib or complain when I don't get the food I want or why I opt to visit out-of-the-way towns instead of heading to exotic locales or why I don't mind the blisters on my feet or the snotty children, the heat or the mosquitos, the drunken bar brawls, the endless mindless talks…I enjoy every bit of this.

I don't know if I do this out of a desire to break the monotony of life or a careless need to stir up something out of the ordinary because in doing them is my freedom. My agenda is never made up of picture opportunities that can be later posted on Facebook or Twitter or Instagram. Yes, I like to take pictures and I look at them longingly and lovingly later on but I don't live to see the world through my camera lens.

I am yet to understand why people find it strange that they constantly meet others who have visited the exact same country as themselves, often also the same places or towns—why strange I wonder. There are two hundred and forty-five countries in the world and it goes without saying that people wander about within these countries.

Travel has made me more aware and tolerant and extended my limits of patience. As a traveller, I have been the vagabond, greedy, poor, giver, receiver, curious and indifferent, lustful and insensitive, shy and bold, self-centred and calm—I have been all that, yet I know I fit into a category. Much as I like to flatter myself into believing I am a unique kind of traveller, I know the category I speak about exists and is definitive. There is a traveller's ritual that somehow makes us bond, behave in a similar fashion, leading us to the same tracks and sometimes creating similar memories.

Agreed, I do tend to get a little frustrated when I am asked about being 'Indian' as though such a breed of travellers don't exist, but over the years I have got used to it. There are times when you tend to get a little fed up with these conversations because, well, there are so many times when you want to feel like an alien species, but it is something you endure and shrug and move on.

An incredible number of people are travelling to see the world, a majority of them however typically end up in beaches, bars, pubs and shopping malls. They get a driver's licence, parachute from planes, bungee jump off bridges. They go rafting and meet other travellers with the same mindset who are running the same track, doing the same stuff, exchange stories and then return thinking they have seen the world. They have, yes, except they are seeing the same world they knew from back home.

I travel a little slow and hope that what I have learnt can be of some use to others. This book is about specific journeys and how to travel in general. I have conducted successful and some not-so-successful experiments and have tried to find answers.

The truth however remains that no matter where we come from and where we go, we are all unknown travellers. Yes. I just said that. I think this is good. As long as we learn to accept the universal traveller's truth, we will be fine as travellers. Whether going from one town to the next, one country to the next, we are unknown. True, we may strike up conversations and make friendships, some long-lasting and some not, but we are basically people in transit. We take back what we see and experience or what others show to us, then we move on.

Being unknown perhaps helps to discover a deeper meaning into our existence—I am not sure. What I am sure is that we are 'unknowns'. Maybe we choose to be unknown because there are no boundaries and there are no limits. We are given a clean slate every time we visit a new city, town or village. We become the person with no name.

Maybe.

Travel allows me to submit to the unfamiliar, to live out my desire for the unknown, to live the 'paradise on earth' fantasies, to test myself in unfamiliar circumstances, to prove that I can do anything that my heart desires.

Travel signifies change. It gives me an opportunity to eat new things, experience new sensations—adventure in Amazon, awe in Gobi, desperation in North Korea, pampering in Bali, emotions in Africa…

I love travelling. Period. I refuse to be too careful and thereby miss the excitement that would otherwise have been mine. The essential part of my journey is getting to know myself and my strengths and limits of adaptability. So what if I get sick? I get sick at home, too. I am okay with getting sick. As long as I don't die of it, I feel pretty good about my decisions. If I did die, well, I have nothing to worry about, right?

I bond with people better when I am on the roads. I understand better. I am more focused. Travelling is that subtle factor that connects me to people, helps me explore the differences and encourages me to accept the world as it is.

How we treat our world, the environment, other people's countries and cultures, and how we treat other people as we travel, is very important. Have I always got it right? No. But I try. And when I fail, I'm sometimes able to rectify my error.

Currently, I'm transitioning from my backpacker identity to a traveller and writer and to ease through the stage I'm experiencing what's called the 'eternal bewilderment of sorts'. I have no idea what that means, but it goes well with the identity I want to create.

Funnily enough, each time I return or when someone in the media asks me a question, it is always so limiting: 'What was your favourite place?' 'What was your favourite moment?' 'Food?' 'Tell us one incident that made the travel special?'

I want to say that I have more than one favourite food and place. I have many stories to tell. The 'non-travellers' don't get it. Travels are made up of more than one story, they are little stories weaved into one big exciting journey. My stories, stories of people I meet, the story behind that hammock in the sun, the story of the woman who sold me her coat...travel has helped me gather stories about everything and everyone. It has made me observe and thereby made me understand the world a little better.

When I return from my travels, in my mind's eye I see a changing pattern of colours, smells, sights and sounds. I see the warmth and love of the locals, the thrill of being out in the sun, of freezing in the cold, of drinking tea with strangers...the lack of fear, the sheer joy. Being a solo female traveller is nothing to fear.

And I move on. I leave one place even if it is a place I want to live in forever. Like Trabzon. Like Nairobi. Like Ulan Baatar. Because deep down I know I have to be somewhere else.

...So I Travel.

ACKNOWLEDGEMENTS

...And hereby I acknowledge every little thing you guys did that made my travels memorable.

To Avinash and Maneesh for always treating me like a 'bro'.

To Safak Deniz. To whom I owe my initiative Travel & Relief.

To İbrahim Çavuşoğlu for instilling faith in couchsurfing. Deborah Luo for forcing me to learn to eat with chopsticks. Katarzyna Pawlak, Lawrence Cenotto and Valerie Menenberg for the happy evenings in North Korea. Irene Tsai and Eren Komurlu for that one wonderful evening in Trabzon.

To my fantastic guide without whom I'd still be lost in the Gobi Desert. Doljmaa Songorov for suggesting that fantastic guide and Stella in Uganda for the free rides in her government car.

To all those people whom I met on my travels – THANK YOU for the moments of togetherness, for smiles, for unbilled drinks, for free rides and to strangers who watched out for my well-being.

To Ms Deer from North Korea whose beautiful voice still haunts me – for her song *Aarirang*.

To Rohit Jayakaran who still thinks I can use technology to make life better and for his award-winning 1 Minute ideas, coffee and for being absolutely sure he'll watch a film based on my book one day.